Theory for Theatre Studies: Emotion

Theory for Theatre Studies meets the need for accessible, mid-length volumes that unpack keywords that lie at the core of the discipline. Aimed primarily at undergraduate students and secondarily at postgraduates and researchers, volumes feature both background material historicizing the term and original, forward-looking research into intersecting theoretical trends in the field. Case studies ground volumes in praxis, and additional resources online ensure readers are equipped with the necessary skills and understanding as they move deeper into the discipline.

SERIES EDITORS

Susan Bennett, University of Calgary, Canada
Kim Solga, Western University, Canada

Published titles
Theory for Theatre Studies: Space
Kim Solga
Theory for Theatre Studies: *Sound*
Susan Bennett
Theory for Theatre Studies: Memory
Milija Gluhovic

Forthcoming titles
Theory for Theatre Studies: Bodies Soyica Diggs Colbert
Theory for Theatre Studies: Movement Rachel Fensham
Theory for Theatre Studies: Economics Michael McKinnie
Theory for Theatre Studies: Aesthetics John Lutterbie

Theory for Theatre Studies: Emotion

Peta Tait

Series editors: Susan Bennett and Kim Solga

methuen | drama

LONDON • NEW YORK • OXFORD • NEW DELHI • SYDNEY

METHUEN DRAMA
Bloomsbury Publishing Plc
50 Bedford Square, London, WC1B 3DP, UK
1385 Broadway, New York, NY 10018, USA

BLOOMSBURY, METHUEN DRAMA and the Methuen Drama logo are
trademarks of Bloomsbury Publishing Plc

First published in Great Britain 2021

Series design by Louise Dugdale
Cover image © Henrik Sorensen/Photodisc/Getty

A catalogue record for this book is available from the British Library.

A catalog record for this book is available from the Library of Congress.

ISBN:　　HB:　　978-1-3500-3085-5
　　　　　PB:　　978-1-3500-3084-8
　　　　　ePDF:　978-1-3500-3087-9
　　　　　eBook:　978-1-3500-3086-2

Series: Theory for Theatre Studies

Typeset by Integra Software Services Pvt. Ltd.
Printed and bound in Great Britain

To find out more about our authors and books visit www.bloomsbury.com
and sign up for our newsletters.

CONTENTS

SERIES PREFACE

Theory for Theatre Studies (TfTS) is a series of introductory theoretical monographs intended for both undergraduate and postgraduate students as well as researchers branching out into fresh fields. It aims to introduce constellations of ideas, methods, theories and rubrics central to the working concerns of scholars in theatre and performance studies at the opening of the twenty-first century. With a primary focus on twentieth-century developments, TfTS volumes offer accessible and provocative engagements with critical theory that inspire new ways of thinking theory in important disciplinary and interdisciplinary modes.

The series features full-length volumes explicitly aimed at unpacking sets of ideas that have coalesced around carefully chosen key terms in theatre and performance, such as space, sound, bodies, memory, movement, economies and emotion. TfTS volumes do not aggregate existing essays, but rather provide a careful, fresh synthesis of what extensive reading by our authors reveals to be key nodes of interconnection between related theoretical models. The goal of these texts is to introduce readers to a wide variety of critical approaches and to unpack the complex theory useful for both performance analysis and creation.

Each volume in the series focuses on one specific set of theoretical concerns, constellated around a term that has become central to understanding the social and political labour of theatre and performance work at the turn of the millennium. The organization of each book follows a common template: Section One includes a historical overview of interconnected theoretical models, Section Two features extended case studies using twentieth- and twenty-first-century performances and

Section Three looks ahead, as our authors explore important new developments in their constellation. Each volume is broad enough in scope to look laterally across its topic for compelling connections to related concerns, yet specific enough to be comprehensive in its assessment of its particular term. The ideas explored and explained through lively and detailed case studies provide diverse critical approaches for reading all kinds of plays and performances as well as starting points for practical exploration.

Each book includes a further reading section and features a companion website with chapter summaries, questions for discussion, and a host of video and other web links.

Susan Bennett (University of Calgary, Canada)
and Kim Solga (Western University, Canada)

ACKNOWLEDGEMENTS

I want to thank Mark Dudgeon at Methuen Drama and the series editors of *Theory for Theatre Studies*, Susan Bennett and Kim Solga, for the invitation to contribute to this forward-looking innovative book series and for their careful attention and thoughtful suggestions during the writing process. This opportunity allowed me to explore aspects of theatre and performance that I have long found fascinating, in an accessible account of the emotions and affect. I continue to find emotion evocative but mercurial as it defies description in language. My sincere thanks to Professor Elizabeth Schafer, Emeritus Professor Julie Holledge and Dr Kim Baston for generously taking time out of busy schedules to provide invaluable comments on an earlier draft. I have benefitted greatly from the work of my performance studies colleagues and our conversations over years, and my connections with the ARC Centre of Excellence for the History of Emotions. A big thank you to Dr Diane Carlyle and La Trobe University's DRP research assistance. Heartfelt thanks as always to Annie McGuigan for patiently reading my work with such engaged attention.

Author's note: filmed performances are described in the past tense to accord with the standard approach for live performance, while plays are discussed in present tense.

Introduction:
Approach and concepts

Emotions have an impact everywhere in life. This does not mean that they are easily explained. An emotional declaration such as 'I love you' is vague, even unreliable because the English word 'love' has multiple meanings and the declaration needs a context. This is where theatrical performance comes to the fore. Dramatic scripts present narratives that frame the emotions in a context, and theatrical performance conveys some of the accompanying physical and physiological dimensions.

Theatrical performance in Western culture has always presented and interpreted the emotions of individuals, families and social interactions in recognizable ways even within the context of extreme events. But in a philosophy of emotion, Carolyn Price is careful to point out that emotions are diverse and only approximately similar (Price 2015: 6). Since emotions are experienced in a range of ways, there needs to be social opportunities to align them. In communicating about the emotions, drama and theatrical performance encourage thinking about them and interpretations of their development and veracity. Price elaborates that 'an emotional response, then, is not just a matter of *feeling* a certain way: it can involve thinking, wanting, remembering, and imagining; it can involve changes in your body and in your behaviour' (2015: 2, italics in original). The possibilities for thinking about and remembering emotion, as well as imagining it, have long been part of theatre and its theory and practice. The emotions of theatrical performance contribute to social experience.

Emotion investigates dramatic narratives and performance processes that invite shared understanding as it asks: what does performance communicate about emotion and why is this important? The book presents four concepts that are widely used – the emotions, emotional feelings, affect and mood – to explain what happens in theatrical performance. *Emotion* points out that the emotions and emotional feelings should be distinguished as happens in other disciplinary fields of study, and that affect and emotional feeling can be separated out in theatrical patterns of engagement, patterns that additionally create an overarching emotional mood. In this book, the emotions are cognitive ideas and impressions, emotional feelings are physiological experiences, and affect emphasizes embodied felt sensitivity to and within the surroundings while the concept of mood allows individual, social and aesthetic experiences to be linked.

A shorthand way of separating these concepts within lived experience involves allocating duration. Affect is short-lived and transient happening in seconds, emotional feeling lasts minutes and has the potential to last hours whereas an individual mood can last days, even months, and the emotions are spoken about in language over years.

Applied to theatrical performance (Hurley 2010: 22–3), the four concepts encapsulate the different functions involved with creating and watching it. The diverse perspectives operating within live performance can include those of a writer, a director, the performers, the musicians, designers and technological artists, as well as those of audience members. Performance-makers approach emotion in relation to a specialized capacity: a writer will compile words for the emotions in a text which a performer speaks and seeks to embody as emotional feeling, and a director will consider both cognitive ideas and embodied expression as well as create the overall mood effect working with a music composer and a lighting designer. An audience member will respond cognitively to ideas of the emotions and mood as well as bodily with affect and emotional feeling.

The arousal of audience feeling is a theatrical intention. Erin Hurley's (2010) succinct, insightful summary argues that feeling is central to theatre as she explains, spectators 'attend the theatre to feel *more*, even if it doesn't make us feel *better*; we go to have our emotional life acknowledged and patterned', and potentially 'expanded' (Hurley 2010: 77, italics in original). Hurley explains that theatre helps us interpret our emotional feelings and she describes how spectators respond vicariously to performers and explores a theatrical potential for the transmission of feeling to the spectator. Conversely, Martin Welton contends that it is the whole experience of attending live performance which creates spectator feeling because it arises from being in a designated space (ecology) with all its elements (2012: 8). These different explanations of how feeling happens in theatrical performance point to multiple types of felt experience.

From comedy to serious drama, emotions are an inseparable part of the communication in theatrical performance whether directly through words for the emotions or through more indirect effects such as emotional feeling, affect and mood; these are introduced in this Introduction. *Emotion* has three main sections that explore how contrasting dramatic genres and live performance present emotion as: ideas of the emotions through the narrative, spoken text and acting in Section One; less tangible affect and emotional feeling and empathy in spectator responses to performance and technologies in Section Two; aesthetic moods of large and intimate productions that interweave subjective and shared experience in Section Three.

Section One, Legacies and Case Studies, explains the communication of emotions: in ancient Greek tragedy, Euripides's *Medea*, and Aristotle's analysis; in Shakespeare's romantic comedy *Twelfth Night*; and in twentieth-century realist drama such as Chekhov's *The Seagull* and Brecht's *The Caucasian Chalk Circle*. This section probes Stanislavski's and Brecht's approaches to acting and the approaches of other influential theatre practitioners and theorists who advocate thinking about the emotions and to benefit society. Section Two, Affect and Case Studies, contrasts the emotional feeling in Henrik Ibsen's psychologically realist play, *A Doll's House*, with sensations of affect evoked by a non realist production such as Mabou Mines's *Dollhouse*. Contemporary performances by Stelarc and Cirque du Soleil illustrate affect theory about impersonal energetic exchange and within technological worlds. More meaningfully, the affect of real life converges with the affect of political performance in the work of Anna Deavere Smith. Drama and performance focused on gender, racial and sexual (LGBTQI) identity, disability, and Indigenous First Nations identity, however, invite empathy and other personal responses to stories of suffering such as those presented in Jane Harrison's *Stolen*. All encompassing performances, such as Robert Lepage's *Needles and Opium* and *887*, evoke affect, emotional feeling and empathy. Section Three, Mood and Case Studies, explores and contrasts how the production of aesthetic mood connects to individual mood in 'feel-good' musicals such as *The Lion King* and *Dear Evan Hansen* about friendship and in intense immersive performance such as *The Artist Is Present* by Marina Abramovic. It explores political economies of mood in *Alladeen* and the ambient productions of Socìetas Raffaello Sanzio, Rimini Protokoll and The Wooster Group. As Section Three considers eco-moods of fear in productions about the future, it outlines how a happier mood can emerge from the anticipation of performance – its future promise.

Emotion draws on studies of theatre and refers to studies of the emotions in science, philosophy, psychology and sociology, some of which ask the underlying question: what is an emotion? The answers are open-ended because responses vary according to the discipline, and disciplinary study of theatre contains its own variation. A scientific study considers biological brain activity, while a sociological explanation might emphasize the emotions in social exchange and a psychological explanation might emphasize individual emotional feeling (e.g. Harré and Parrott 1996). Like theatre, philosophy is often concerned with the relationship between ethical values and the emotions (Goldie 2012b). Only performance, however, repeatedly shows the ways in which the emotions are performed in society. The process of performing emotions in lifelike ways became particularly refined within early-twentieth-century realist theatre (Tait 2002). Theatrical and screen performance suggests that we copy the emotions around us in our social worlds. Performance often presents emotions with logical causes that align with, even influence, widely accepted psychological frameworks but such emotional expression may also reinforce social stereotypes. Social beliefs about emotion are interpreted through performance and its aesthetic styles, and therefore identity diversity in innovative performance needs to be supported by emotion (Tait forthcoming).

In *Emotion*, the emotions, emotional feelings, affect and mood are conceived of within a spectrum and as conditions that overlap and flow into each other. The four concepts are introduced in the summaries below, which encompass related terms including empathy and their historical antecedents. They are explored in detail through the case studies and other examples of drama, theatre and performance in the book's three sections.

The emotions

Drama communicates the emotions through words and language and draws on a long history within which particular emotions have remained recognizable. The ancient Greek philosopher Aristotle describes an audience thinking about the emotions presented in the narrative and its dramatic action, and responding with pity and fear which remain recognizable today (see Section One). A dramatic narrative presents the emotions of, for example, love, grief, anger and fear as inspiring characters or causing upheavals and having detrimental consequences in their lives. Drama depicts the emotions shaping social interaction as a character's disgust or embarrassment or jealousy is conveyed through verbal disclosure and exchanges between characters.

While an audience member might recognize a word for an emotion – the social idea of an emotion – this is not the same as having a corresponding emotional feeling. Love or anger refers to what is broadly understood about that emotion and there are hundreds of words in English used in communication and thinking. In addition, language in communication is accompanied by structures that qualify and allow for tone and vocal expression to enhance the meaning of the words, and theatre effectively reproduces and highlights the intonations of social languages.

In theatre and in philosophy over millennia, the emotions were interpreted through thought and cognition, and it was assumed mental functions preceded emotional feeling. While the words are shorthand in everyday communication for an all-pervasive feeling that can become overwhelming, the study of the emotions requires more careful distinctions. Neuroscientist Antonio Damasio explains that the 'emotions and feelings are not the same thing as objects of study', although they are brought together in 'real life' (2004: 49). He explains that studies of emotion confirm 'distinctive, albeit interrelated, physiological and mental events that benefit from separate designations' and 'allow for a clearer communication' (Damasio 2004: 50).

The emotions have been well studied in theatre. Joseph Roach (1985) explains that historically actors were considered to have specialist knowledge about the emotions, which were formerly called passions. The word 'emotion' comes from a Latin word, *emovere*, about vitality and means 'to move out, to stir up' (Roach 1985: 27). But it probably came into the English language through the French *esmovoir*, and means '"to remove, displace"', to 'disturb' even dislocate (Jensen and Wallace 2015: 1249). A range of meanings suggesting movement reflects how theatrical performance emotionally moves an audience and how feeling is changeable, shifting in focus and scope and expanding and contracting. As Katharine Jensen and Miriam Wallace point out, however, dictionary definitions of the emotions (words) can be misleading when these start with the premise of 'individual self-possession' of an object, so that an explanation applied to what is happening in literature (and in theatre) does not encompass a fluctuating experience inseparable from the artistic and social context (2015: 1252).

Particular emotions such as love, anger, fear and shame might remain recognizable over millennia but their collective noun label changes over that time. The word 'emotion' appeared in the English language in the seventeenth century, and it was increasingly used in the eighteenth century coming into common usage as the collective term for individual emotions during the nineteenth century and to gradually replace earlier words such as 'sensibility', 'sentiment' and 'passion' (Fisher 2002: 6–7; Roach 1985: 95). Sentiment was connected to sensibility which reflected a historically specific belief evident in literature, philosophy and science from the mid-eighteenth-century about, 'an innate ability to experience readily and intensely a broad spectrum of emotions, perceptions, and sensations, but especially a kind of tender, pleasurable sorrow' (Kastan 2006). By the nineteenth century, 'sentimental' referred to superficial or insincere expression of emotion. Sensation came into use from the 1860s to describe literature and theatre that depicted sensationalist events such as crimes, murder and the secrets of 'transgressive women', and although the characters and their actions were morally questionable within the prevailing values, they were a source of social fascination (Kastan 2006). The word 'emotional' referring to an 'emotional feeling' developed in the nineteenth century, replacing sensibility, and it was increasingly used during the twentieth century.

It is clear that the labelling terms for emotion expand and change as the qualities and meanings are adjusted over time.

Affect offers a complicated example of this change since the philosophical use of affect originally described rage, shame or terror, but over centuries this became diluted to a milder emotional feeling such as affection (Fisher 2002: 4) and, most recently, became detached from emotional feeling. Teresa Brennan writes that 'the term "affect" is one translation of the Latin *affectus*, which also translated as "passion"' (2004: 3). Philip Fisher explains that passion historically was first used in English to mean the extreme emotions of the sufferings of Christ on the cross (2002: 4). He explains that passion meant strong emotion and specifically anger in ancient Greece but that it has come to be used in everyday contemporary language for an enthusiasm or for sexual desire (Fisher 2002: 5). In relation to performance, Roach explains that passion, derived from the Latin *patior* meaning to suffer, was linked to historical understanding of the body and scrutinized for the ways in which it might be imaginatively, facially and gesturally replicated by a speaker (actor) to induce sympathetic feeling in audiences (1985: 28). The process of analysing and defining the emotions and terms continues to be relevant to the practice of theatre. Theatrical delivery was and is bound up with thought and a linguistic approach to the emotions, and it has responded and does respond to changing belief about the emotions.

Emotional feelings

The accepted convention is that theatrical performance evokes the feelings of audience members. Since these are experienced through the body, its physiological processes are implicated. Audience feeling might be guided by, for example, the narrative, the accompanying signs such as a label of comic or tragic, the performance, the music and the technical effects. As performers present nonverbal facial and bodily indicators of emotional feelings with spoken language, they illustrate how emotional feeling is understood, observed and perceived. While anger or love can be communicated by a performer in nonverbal ways, other emotions such as envy or paranoia can seem ambiguous to spectators without words, and some emotions are not socially accorded facial expression. In the absence of words, audience interpretation of which particular emotional feeling is being enacted might diverge even with agreement that the performance is emotional or intense.

The interpretation of other people's feeling in everyday life is often ambiguous – as it can be in theatre. For example, involuntary blushing might suggest someone is embarrassed when he or she (they) could be angry. Embodied feeling, however, develops in familiar patterns within families and everyone has the capacity for emotional feeling, which is also shared with nonhuman species. The triggering of adult human emotional feelings is associated with the amygdala, a small area in the base of the brain. The scientific study of electrochemical patterns of emotional feelings locates them, as Damasio shows, in several areas of the brain often simultaneously, and particularly in the older parts, in the brain stem, hypothalamus that releases chemicals and peptides, and especially the amygdala in the temporal lobe and ventromedial prefrontal cortex (2003: 59). Sections of the frontal lobe including the ventromedial prefrontal area integrate emotions, memory and sensory experience in meaningful ways. Some parts of the brain, however, do seem to correspond with particular emotional feelings; feelings of fear may or may not arise in the amygdala while emotions such as embarrassment are connected across areas. The physiology of emotional feelings is complex because it encompasses desires, happening in multiple regions of the brain and throughout the body in rapid succession, and responding in part to sensory input and thought. Rick Kemp (2012) explains that recent brain science provides valuable knowledge for performers. Psychologist

Lisa Feldman Barrett (2018) supports emotional intelligence training as she argues that physiology may be shaped more by life experience than hard-wired and that the flexible brain learns to predict an emotional feeling as meaningful within a context.

Interestingly, human feeling is described in psychological studies with terms used in theatre such as roles or 'emotion scripts' or 'social scripts' (Tompkins 1995; Parkinson, Fischer and Manstead 2005: 41, 44). Psychologist Silvan Tomkins (1995) describes emotional feeling with a combination of words such as fear-terror or distress-anguish that signify compounding experiences which are difficult to reduce to a word. Theatrical performance confirms that one emotion replaces another when, for example, an unexpected occurrence initially causes surprise that turns into fear. It reveals fluctuations in emotional responses towards other people, the situation, events, nonhuman others and inanimate objects.

In the late nineteenth century, William James with Carl Lange (1967) questioned the prevailing belief in the study of emotion that feeling followed thought by arguing physiological changes precede conscious thinking. The separation of an idea of an emotion from an emotional feeling ensued, and arguments developed in the twentieth century about whether an emotional feeling is self-generated or happens in response to external occurrences. The influential challenge to James's (1984) sequence of bodily feeling before mental processing comes from appraisal theory that finds feeling develops in relation to external stimuli and cognition, even where someone is not consciously aware of the orientation (Lazarus 1994; Frijda 1994). (Theatrical performance provides external stimuli for spectator feeling.) Towards the end of the twentieth century, neuroscience shows that the brain activity of feeling happens seconds prior to conscious thought – these studies utilize external images and provocations. Science suggests that the neurobiology of the brain-body reacts rapidly to the surroundings.

As Stephen Di Benedetto (2010) explains, sensory perception and how the brain responds to facial expressions are relevant to theatrical performance. He outlines automatic correspondences in emotional feelings such as disgust between people (2010: 14). Di Benedetto explains that brain patterns are laid down through repetition, which leads to recognition and the arousal of compatible feeling. But a repetitive pattern of sensory engagement can also bypass an emotionally felt response. There is a philosophical argument that the definition of a feeling refers to a bodily condition that is consciously apprehended (Damasio 2004: 52; Kemp 2012). Therefore, the contemporary use of affect to describe bodily sensation provides a useful distinction from emotional feeling that fuels individual behaviour or simply involves self-reflective awareness.

In general, audiences respond to how performance surrounds them with clues about how to feel. Audiences attending a comedy are predisposed to being amused, and feel freer to laugh and to presume that others find comic action funny. At the same time, a vocal reaction such as laughter is observed by artists, and other audience members, as an outward indicator of mirth. But audience members may find themselves laughing because others in the audience are laughing, as if caught up in a type of involuntary reflex reaction. A response can be accentuated by the reactions of a group and can be contagious. Conversely, an amused audience member might hesitate to laugh out loud among a silent crowd. (The word 'amusement' ranges from the bodily sensation of affect to emotional feeling.) A degree of voluntary control over outward reactions is apparent.

A performer will be performing anger rather than feeling it, because he or she (they) cannot afford to be overcome with anger even where its expression draws on rehearsed processes involving feeling (see Section One), and a spectator will recognize that angry feelings are being represented without becoming angry. Therefore, theatrical performance suggests: firstly, it is possible to present and recognize distinctive emotional feelings without feeling them or reciprocating with similar feeling; secondly, feeling exists within a spectrum of voluntary to involuntary responses. There can be variable levels of control arising with awareness of feeling – performers learn ways to manage feeling in their training.

Analysis of the reception of performance from the 1980s recognizes the importance of factors external to the performance and that socio-economic background often determines the composition of audiences. As Susan Bennett explains, there are a 'range of production objectives and ideologies at work in mainstream and other theatres' which 'determine – at least in part – the characteristics of the audiences which are likely to attend' (1990: 123). Along with social background, theories of reception recognize that a spectator brings perspectives based on cultural difference to performance interpretation; that is, a spectator's subjective responses are influenced by experiences of race, ethnicity, gender and sexuality. Lived experience impacts on felt responses to performance (Dolan 2008). The emotionally felt responses of spectators can be influenced by personal and cultural backgrounds, which include prior theatrical experience.

Affect and its theory

Affect is a noun, a product of a process of feeling (Brennan 2004: 23). Affect in *Emotion* refers to embodied felt sensation (pulses, tingles, auras, slight involuntary movements) and bodily sensitivity to and within the surroundings, and it includes the sensation accompanying thought. Affect in theatrical performance is being distinguished in this discussion from emotional feeling to broaden the explanation of the overall scope of artistic emotion and to allow for personal responses. In turn, the distinction illuminates some of the significant theoretical points about affect which are briefly introduced below.

The longstanding association of affect with emotional feeling has been decoupled in the twenty-first century. An enlarged significance envisaged by the theorists of affect means that affect and emotional feeling are no longer simply interchangeable. Affect is the most complicated term used here because it highlights sensory perception and covers a myriad of reactions, and there is confusion evident in applications of affect theory to performance, and it becomes necessary to ask if 'affect' is being used in its expanded theoretical interpretation or refers to an older equivalence with emotional feeling. Bridget Escolme adopts a useful strategy of referring to 'emotional affect' (2014: xiv).

Affect has become a central concept in the analysis of what is being sensorily and bodily felt and thought in theatre and performance, which highlights one aspect of its current theoretical interpretation. In categories of affect, only one of eight refers to emotional feeling, and because affect theory argues against the idea of a self-contained intrinsic self (Gregg and Seigworth 2010). Affect offers ideas of a porous body that responds to energetic movement, which is also applicable to theatrical experience and its technologies (see Section Two). Performance induces bodily sensations as well as emotional feelings and I have written elsewhere in detail about the visceral bodily impact of circus acrobatic performance, and Hurley also uses circus to explain the bodily 'thrills' of performance (Hurley 2010: 13). Acrobatic action, which is the basis of circus, invites an involuntary bodily response; feeling might involve a voluntary or involuntary physiological change.

In her influential psychoanalytical writing Brennan explains, 'the things that one feels are affects. The things that one feels with are feelings' (2004: 23). Brennan's explanation of 'to feel' (love) means feeling and affective responses are active, associated with verbs (2004: 23). This suits theatrical purposes although Brennan is applying affect within a therapeutic context.

Affect in performance, however, is challenging to describe as it is an indirect effect of the process of bodily pulses and physiological processes. Such sensations are immediate but seem short-lived, difficult to sustain through awareness. In addition, affect theory extrapolates on how feeling surrounds bodies, and involves energetic leaps between bodies, as it contends affect is not personally possessed. In this expanded meaning, affect is no longer equated with individual feeling and can be summarized as referring either to human sensitivity to the invisible and intangible energetic change of bodies or to nonhuman flows and currents. Recognition of the arousal of affect in theatrical performance has been sparked by a number of theoretical approaches summarized as the 'turn to affect' or the 'affective turn' in humanities scholarship suggesting a 'new configuration of bodies, technology and matter' (Clough 2007b: 2). Brian Massumi (2002) describes affect as sensitivity to energetic movement and what moves beyond the visible surroundings, which can be felt bodily. Thus affective energy can be continuous and happening regardless of attentive thought. Affect has 'autonomy', by which Massumi means energetic fields move across bodies and beyond them and are expansive and open rather than bodily contained (2002: 35). These theories of affect are connected to the philosophy of Gilles Deleuze and his interpreters, conceptualizing what surrounds and underlies material culture in energetic flows and exchanges (Massumi 2002: 32–3). Patricia Clough writes that 'affect refers generally to bodily capacities' or feelings which are linked to 'aliveness or vitality' (2007b: 2). Ideas of affect hold philosophical significance in relation to being alive. Accordingly, concepts of energetic sensation and aliveness nominated by affect theory can be aligned with well-established concepts of the live and liveness in theory about performance, and intangible exchanges happening during live performance (Phelan 1993; Heathfield 2004; Parker-Starbuck 2011: 9). These philosophical ideas of the live in performance refer to the theatrical premise that the performer(s) and spectator(s) are in a physical space (or digital space) at the same time and for a set duration; the ideas point to feeling alive in the moment. The vitality of the live exchange in performance aligns with concepts of affect.

By denoting flow and connection, affect removes the separation, for example, between thought and bodily feeling. In writing about aesthetics, Lauren Berlant (2011) expands the idea of 'affect' into that of an event that develops through the body's experience of its surroundings. The body becomes characterized as an entity of 'movement and process' in an ontology of becoming and, as Lisa Blackman explains, affect then refers to experience that is 'non-cognitive, trans-subjective, non-conscious, non-representational, incorporeal and immaterial' (2012: 1, 3). As she explains, however, concepts of affect arising from a body's autonomic systems and through contagion exist independently from histories of psychology and personality and therefore also individual experience of emotional feeling.

Significantly then, affect theory eschews ideas of a personal self who possesses emotional feeling. Massumi is interested in rethinking the function of power in the twenty-first century and exploring new interpretations of affect as energy that permeates social intention and the state, and operates within its virtual spaces. Michael Hardt (2007) suggests that affect theory emerges from efforts to synthesize body, mind, reason and passion that go back to the philosopher Baruch Spinoza and continue in a current practical consideration of '*affective labor*' (2007: xi, italics in original). Clough (2007b) explains how recent theory about affect developed in combination with major changes in economic ideas of work, global capitalism and the impact of digital technology on all aspects of life. She points out that these changed conditions required a broader explanation that is social and not reducible to individual subjectivity (Clough 2007b: 3). Affective labour can be found in the computerized virtual transactions of the twenty-first-century digital economy, which diverge from the twentieth-century concept of 'emotion work' in person-to-person service industries. Digital services can be impersonal. Older ideas about the hierarchical structures of capitalism and the means of material production became inadequate when faced with the expansive shift brought about by technologies operating in the horizontal virtual sphere of the digital economy, and as this expanded globally to overshadow national geographies.

Affect theory expanding on Deleuze's ideas of intangible flow can be found in a myriad of interdisciplinary applications (Gregg and Seigworth 2010). These encompass human relations with the nonhuman world and insights from science. Throughout the twentieth century, knowledge was enlarged by science about the composition of the invisible world and microscopic living cells that defy containment. Hence affect theory offers ways of thinking about how the living biological human is enmeshed within nonhuman matter. Ideas of affect encapsulate the circulation of cellular energy between people and within the material world, and affect theory is closely aligned with what is called 'new materialism' (Bennett 2010; van der Tuin and Dolphijn 2010). Affect theory and new materialism draw on scientific concepts to explore how the human and nonhuman and organic and inorganic are inseparable and energetically interwoven. The theory of affect describes energetic patterns that are impersonal and underlie all life rather than that belonging to an individual. Therefore, an analysis of subjective responses to performance is more productively explained by adding the concepts of emotional feeling and mood.

Mood

'Mood' in *Emotion* encompasses the overall emotional tone or sequence of emotional impressions generated by the combined aesthetic effects of performance. While 'mood' in everyday life refers to individually felt emotional experience that persists, it can also refer to the impact of a theatrical production in which an individual audience member is caught up in a joyous or a melancholic mood. As well, a performance can capture a social mood (see Section Three). Theatrical mood denotes an emotional condition that is overarching and less focused than a specific emotion. For example, a character describing a specific emotional feeling might say, 'I feel angry', and he or she might be described as being in an angry mood by another character, while a theatrical production might be described as generating a mood of hostility or threat.

In an analysis of the traits of individuals, Peter Goldie makes a distinction between a longer mood of irritability versus a shorter angry outburst of an emotional feeling (2000: 143). An emotion and an emotional feeling are about something or someone or an event, but individual mood is not so orientated and instead suggests a condition that is described as 'ambient, vague, diffuse, hazy and intangible' (Felski and Fraiman 2012: v). As Robert Roberts explains, the experience of mood does not need reasons or provocations. It can exist and be perceived without verbal acknowledgement when, for example, an individual appears depressed or cheerful (Roberts 2003: 112). Roberts writes that while the emotions and emotional feelings have explanations, someone can experience a mood without it being clearly '*about* anything' (2003: 112, italics in original). But he accepts that moods do have 'causes' due to tiredness or sensory input such as music or even squalid surroundings or concern with the 'state of affairs' that could include political decisions (2003: 112). Mood is not as easily tied to a specific provocation and less reliant on language, and what Roberts terms 'utterance' or verbal explanation, which is central to how others recognize emotional feeling. Significantly, he is pointing out that the surroundings can impact on an individual's psychological mood.

Performance illuminates the impact of surroundings on mood. In many respects, the willing engagement with the aesthetic mood of theatre and film differs from a common definition of individual mood, which can often be unwanted and unable to be discarded and evident either in behaviour or inaction. An artistic mood is intentionally created and sustained; it can be more than the sum of its parts. Mood provides a useful concept with which to describe the varied impact of contemporary live performance, which can be unsettling and disturbing but compelling. An aesthetic mood effect can be emotionally potent and immersive for an audience.

Rita Felski and Susan Fraiman (2012) consider that mood in the arts needs to be theorized and that mood might disrupt or override affect, given that affect is spatially expansive involving energetic flows and movement without visible or aural containment. Mood in performance, for example, can be attributed to the identifiable combination of aesthetic features such as low lighting and saxophone music, whereas affect is not so closely aligned. Felski and Fraiman draw on the tradition of mood in philosophical thought, and specifically, how the philosopher, Martin Heidegger, considers that we are never without mood, and mood emerges within phenomenological awareness of the world. Since mood is considered a fundamental part of the phenomenology of perception (Ratcliffe 2012), it is relevant to the analysis of the phenomenology of performance (Tait 2002; Bleeker, Sherman and Nedelkopoulou 2015). A phenomenology of mood in performance, however, arises with perceptions of its cultural meaning. Felski and Fraiman write: 'If we look back at the history of modern thought, we see that many of its key moods – anxiety, boredom, melancholy – are not only captured in works of philosophy or poetry but are actively promoted and disseminated by these same works' (2012: vi). Theatrical performance can be added here. Felski and Fraiman support the contention that 'moods, then, are often shared, collective, and social, shaping our experience of being with others' (2012: vii). The features of social mood suggest the way that aesthetic mood is experienced.

The theatrical context assists with an interpretation of mood in performance and can be provided by the production elements or a narrative about a social world. In the extreme circumstances of a society at war – for example in Brecht's *The Caucasian Chalk Circle* (see Section One) – the fearful panic of the characters indicates the communal mood. Hence a dramatic depiction of mood might connect a solitary mood and a social mood.

In his analysis of modernist literature of the early twentieth century, Jonathan Flatley (2008) assumes that readers become immersed in a literary mood as he explores the qualities of artistic moods. He explains that depictions of melancholy in artistic works considered classics in culture can be taken as indicative of a writer's response to a mood in society. In reference to recent music and cinema, Ben Highmore reiterates that personal feelings and mood are 'embedded in cultural forms' (2017: 2). He points out that feelings and mood develop in relation to what is created in culture and manifest in tandem with 'material' objects, which are produced by 'labour' and therefore are 'historical' and 'social' (Highmore 2017: 2–3). Popular music and cinema impact on an individual mood, and since these are widely reproduced and accessible, the mood effect is socially shared. Similarly, a mood created in theatrical performance can be shared by its audience. As Flatley explains, however, a characteristic feature of artistic mood is the way it can tantalize and defy an intellectual grasp to seem elusive.

Cultural complexities and empathy

The four concepts presented above allow for cognitive evaluations as well as bodily experience and sensory perception, and they intersect with a number of major concepts in theatre studies. For example, cognition offers an important parallel field of study (McConachie and Hart 2006; Shaughnessy

2013; Blair and Cook 2016). Aspects of space are relevant when theatrical space is simultaneously the physical venue, a symbolic social world, an imagined metaphoric realm (Solga 2019). In addition, theatrical performance creates embodied emotional spaces. Sound is central to the impact of all performance (Bennett 2019). Concepts of emotion align with these ideas, and the interpretation of subjectivity underpinned by psychoanalytical and gender theories, which challenge the privileged subject's dominance through the objectification of the other (Fortier 1997). To some extent a theoretical approach can depersonalize subjectivity, but this is offset in performance analysis by the attention accorded empathy and its ideal of intersubjectivity.

Empathy is considered to arise through thinking and feeling that simulate what another (others) is experiencing. Such a process implicates the function of the imagination as well as intersubjectivity, and performance includes the body (Blair 2009). Definitions of empathy include a mental process, and most, but not all, include emotional feeling (Coplan and Goldie 2011b: xxiii; Cummings 2016). But empathy is commonly associated with experiencing an emotional feeling. An expectation that theatrical performance will induce empathy does not neatly align with ideas of affect in twenty-first-century performance when empathy is associated with a personally felt emotional response. As Amy Coplan and Peter Goldie (2011b) point out, empathy and its precursor, sympathy, were explained through engagement with artworks. The concept of empathy has its own philosophical trajectory back to Robert Vischer's work on art aesthetics in the 1870s and Theodor Lipps's approach, and the phenomenological philosophy of Edmund Husserl and Edith Stein suggesting empathy is involved in experiencing the external world (Coplan and Goldie 2011b: xiii–xv). Its antecedent, sympathy, can be traced back to the eighteenth-century philosopher David Hume, who appreciated that sympathy encouraged an understanding of other people's minds and feelings and for an ethical response (Coplan and Goldie 2011b). Stein elaborates that empathy allows appreciation of the other's consciousness.

Empathy suggests coming close to the experience of another, whereas the associated idea of 'sympathy' means appreciating the plight of another while remaining separate, and 'pity' denotes feeling sorry for a victim while detached from the circumstances. Empathy, however, avoids evaluative judgement about who is deserving.

Explanations of empathetic concepts can be found in the arts, philosophy and in psychology, and in the ethics of care underlying the health and caring professions. Empathy offers an explanation of altruistic behaviour, such as when humans respond to the distress of another – for example, to a baby's cry or a suffering animal. Such descriptions illuminate empathy in interpersonal communication and within aesthetic interpretation and in scientific knowledge. The neuroscientific study of the brain activity over recent decades explains that neurons become activated in part of the brain when an individual performs a task (Di Benedetto 2010; Umiltà 2017). The same area of the brain becomes activated through the mirror neurons on observing someone doing a comparable task – as can happen in theatre (Kemp 2012). Mirror neuron science has general implications for understanding the function of emotion as it implies that the areas of the brain activated through direct involvement and feeling might also become activated indirectly by observing and appreciating the experience of another, and to include perception of another's suffering and emotional feeling (Coplan and Goldie 2011b: xxviii). Hence an empathetic response can become distressing.

Empathy involves adding a context for the other – one reliant on the imagination of what is happening. Hence it becomes qualified as *'higher-level empathy'* and basic *'lower-level empathy'* (Coplan and Goldie 2011b: xxxiii, italics in original). Goldie's (2011) concept of 'perspective-shifting' finds empathy in the arts constitutes a higher level, whereas involuntary reactions in the brain are considered indicative of lower-level functions. This corresponds to the twentieth-century division between social and basic biological emotional feelings, a division that is disputed because all emotions might be considered to be socially shaped (e.g. Ekman and Davidson 1994a). While it is not easy to separate out subjective experiences of feeling, it might be that someone becomes aware of another's plight because of a feeling such as empathy that focuses attention. It offers a productive concept for performance which has an artistic intention to draw attention to stories and circumstances of disadvantage and suffering.

Theatrical emotion, including empathetic feeling, is artistically evoked so that it belongs to cultural practice in the longstanding argument about whether emotional feeling is more culturally shaped and socially nurtured or more attributable to innate natural biology (e.g. Ekman and Davidson 1994a). The performer embodies socially recognizable visual and verbal indicators of emotional experience in speech, tone, facial and bodily expression. But where the acting of emotions in theatre is assumed to reveal a performer's inner experience rather than imitative expression, it reinforces social belief in a self-contained self (Tait 2002: 136). It infers that emotional feeling is innate. As Sara Ahmed explains, the emotions are not in the individual or in the social world but 'allow the individual and the social to be delineated as if they are objects', which contributes to the politics of emotions (2004: 10). Emotions 'create the very effect of the surfaces and boundaries that allow us to distinguish an inside and outside in the first place' (Ahmed 2004: 10). Performance illustrates the politics of the emotions when it prefigures power relations in society. As Jensen and Wallace explain, Western culture considers the mind superior to the body and emotion, and corporeal control over the emotions extends to control over the lives of other people deemed inferior, 'slaves, women, homosexuals, ethnic or raced others' (2015: 1255). The social separation of emotion contributed to the suppression of others, and theatrical performance offers depictions of such impositions. Most cultures have beliefs that socially contextualize emotions within positive and negative values (Parkinson, Fischer and Manstead 2005: 45–6). Western theatre also reflects the positive and negative consequences of emotional practices within culture.

In relation to digital technologies and emotions and the effort to reconcile two parallel fields of affect and the politics of emotion, Adi Kuntsman explains the emotional presence of a screen image can become an object of feeling as well as a subject of viewer feeling, and personal identification with it can create on-line communities (2012: 5–6). But on-line emotional feeling can also be fake. As theatre has long revealed through acting, there is no certainty that a particular emotional feeling is being felt by a performer (or person on-line) and this was a major reason for the condemnation of theatre and actors historically.

A study of emotion and affect on the internet explains that there is a difference between the emotion in a performance that is globally accessible and the everyday responses viewed at a local level and this gap is difficult to map (Garde-Hansen and Gorton 2013: 19–20). Some emotions are culturally specific, and Tim Lomas (2019) has compiled a dictionary of words that describe an emotion in one culture that has no equivalent in other cultures. Richard Shweder (2004), working in the field of cultural psychology, investigates major differences between the cultures and in the expression of emotional feelings and practices and beliefs about emotions, which do not translate easily between cultures. He gives the example of how the death of a child in some cultures does not involve visible signs of sadness such as tears but instead involves bodily symptoms of sickness (Shweder 2004: 89).

Emotion is approached here from the perspective of Western theatre, and how emotion might or might not translate between cultures is beyond the scope of a short single authored book. I was part of a Korean-Australian project, 'An Intercultural Study of Performing Bodies and Emotions', from 2002–4, and I had to revise my assumptions that a realist production of an Australian play in Korea would be understood by Korean performers and audiences in comparable ways (see Tait and Shim 2006). Not only did a play about a mother reunited with her adult daughter forcibly adopted at birth acquire a completely different symbolic meaning about family separation between North Korea and South Korea, as Jung-Soon Shim explains, the play's emotional dynamics were interpreted through *Han*, the Korean sense of resentful tragic loss (Tait and Shim 2006). Importantly, this project did confirm that a culturally different script can be rewarding because of what performers and spectators from another culture bring to the interpretation and engagement.

Emotion considers the ways in which drama and theatrical performance align with other disciplinary approaches while revealing some unique perspectives. Theoretical approaches discussed here contend that the emotional feelings experienced within theatre are not the same as those in life while recognizing that they intersect and illuminate what happens; some contemporary performance tries to close this gap. Theatre directors wrestle with the expression of emotion in performance, and the relevance of the theatrical adage 'less is more', to discourage histrionic expression. For example, Aristotle disapproved of excessive display (1987: 74, chapter 26), and Constantin Stanislavski experimented with ways of appearing to suppress emotion in order to seem lifelike, while Robert Lepage criticizes those who set out to act emotional feelings. The physically strenuous productions of Elizabeth LeCompte externalize and objectify emotional feeling and thereby remove it.

The performance of emotion is integrated into dramatic and physical action, so that spectator affect, emotional feeling and mood can seem oblique. There are complex cultural dimensions to how emotion is communicated in performance, explicitly through descriptions of the emotions and implicitly through experiences of affect, emotional feeling and mood.

SECTION ONE

Legacies and case studies

Section One addresses how the emotions have been communicated in dramatic narratives and through acting in theatre. It illustrates the way ideas of the emotions change across three key periods of theatre history: ancient Greece, early modern England and twentieth-century Western theatre. For much of history, theatre has had to conform to prevailing social values about emotional relationships and yet it often managed to surreptitiously challenge propriety. From questioning a mother's love in Euripides's *Medea* and in Brecht's *The Caucasian Chalk Circle* to playful romantic partnerships in Shakespeare's *Twelfth Night*, drama focuses on the emotional bonds of fundamental human relationships.

Aristotle addressed controversies around theatre's depiction of emotionally charged behaviour by championing the value of tragedy but criticizing comedy, whereas the Puritans in early modern England opposed all kinds of stage drama. Aristotle's writing, Greek theatre and Shakespeare's drama are discussed here not only because these continue to be important in contemporary theatre and dramatic theory, but also because they remain central to the philosophical and theatrical interpretation of the emotions. By the twentieth century, however, controversies in theatre had shifted primarily to the acting of emotional feeling. The main approaches derived from Constantin Stanislavski's 'System', including techniques for lifelike acting, proved contentious and were opposed by Bertolt

Brecht's epic theatre advocating stylistic shifts and interludes to prevent an audience becoming emotionally absorbed in the performance.

Aristotle on tragic pity and Euripides's *Medea*

Aristotle proposes that what happens to characters in tragedy stirs feelings of pity (*eleos, oiktos*) for them from the audience, accompanied by fear (*phobos*) about being placed in similar circumstances (Belfiore 1992: 184–6). He explains that the story, the plot of the drama, communicates reasons for the emotions and produces an emotional effect. In this framework, thinking about the emotions progresses to feeling them. The drama of ancient Greece involved interpretations of poetic epics that were theatrically staged including at the City Dionysia, an annual festival held over three days attended by most of the citizens (Green 1994). The performances thereby generated a common understanding shaped by how the emotions were made meaningful within the dramatic narratives. Theatre, however, was controversial at this time because of its emotionally persuasive impact on the audience. Aristotle argues that drama should depict virtuous characters and, while he comments on a range of emotions in his non-theatre writing, his surviving commentary about theatre, *Poetics*, is concerned predominantly with pity and fear. Crucially, Aristotle asserts that both characters and dramatic circumstances need to be recognizable to the audience in order to communicate these emotions.

Aristotle claims that the plot should present what is possible but not strain credibility, and he contrasts the value of simple action in which there is a change of fortune with complex action in which there is a reversal or an accompanying discovery (1987: 45, chapter 10). Pity is aroused when the character is undeserving of the change of circumstances and misfortune. Theatre therefore involves a value judgement about the moral worth of the character because, as Aristotle argues, a bad character will not arouse the audience's pity – though this claim is contestable and especially so by the late twentieth century (see Section Three). The events should concern characters who have strong bonds with each other, and Aristotle argues that even someone who only hears the story can react with pity and fear (1987: 49, chapter 14).

Medea by Euripides, written in 431 BC, illustrates this capacity of the story in its graphic account of murderous action. The play opens with Jason and Medea in exile in Corinth, and Medea expressing her outrage about how Jason has rejected her and their sons to marry the daughter of King Creon in order to gain the throne of Corinth. As events unfold, Medea sends a poisoned robe that kills Creon's daughter, Glauce, and Creon. Perhaps fearful of what will happen to her two sons, Medea decides to kill them. This action is completely chilling irrespective of her complicity in earlier deaths. Euripides, however, does not have Medea punished, and she leaves for Athens protected by a childless Aegeus, having promised to assist him to have children.

The crucial point is that the tragedy is what befalls Jason. While he is horrified by the deaths of Glauce and Creon, more tragically, Jason is a father who must endure the murder of his sons. Medea's abhorrent crime is directed at a father's love for his children and the loss of their future and Jason's bloodline. The effectiveness of the revenge comes from a father's emotional attachment and grief, even though a male who openly expresses an emotion such as grief could appear to undermine his masculine demeanour. Audience members could feel pity for Jason living with his suffering, fearing such an eventuality in their own families. Euripides's version of the myth designates Medea as the killer of her children, and Aristotle would probably have considered her evil. The play, however, offers explanations of the emotions behind her actions. It opens with descriptions of Medea unable to eat and crying all day about losing Jason. Rejected, she wishes to die. Those around her describe her anger. Medea bemoans the difficulties facing women who cannot refuse marriage and face husbands who betray them. She would rather be a soldier than a mother. As Edith Hall points out, she 'repudiates the gender role assigned to her' (2010: 244). She wants to punish Jason for his rejection of her and to maximize his suffering (Euripides 1967: 67–8, lines 231–70). In the Greek legend that is the source for the play, Jason and the Argonauts sailed across the Black Sea in search of the golden fleece of a special ram, and Medea, daughter of the King of Colchis, fell in love with Jason, assisting him in killing her brother and violently stealing the fleece, symbolic of power and wealth. They flee to Jason's homeland but his uncle has usurped him, and Medea revealed her murderous capacity when she tricks the uncle's daughters into killing him, to assist Jason. In Euripides's play, Medea calls Jason a coward and her shameless enemy for failing to acknowledge what she sacrificed for him. Jason, however, claims somewhat unconvincingly that he marries again so they can all live well. He does seem to take Medea's loyal love and extreme actions for granted. He also proposes that it would be easier if a man could get his children other than with women who seek to constrain men through the emotions accompanying sexual relations and can turn '[m]ost hateful' if relations cease (Euripides 1967: 77, lines 573–5). Medea sends her sons with the poisoned gown for the new bride and then kills her children because 'there is none who can give them safety' (Euripides 1967: 86, line 793).

Jason may seem emotionally obligated to Medea and fear the force of her vindictive rage, but he does not predict its consequences. Euripides attributes Medea's motives to Jason's disloyalty and broken promise to her – and to their children. Clearly, Medea's actions go against how the emotions are divided up in society with a mother's love elevated and sacrosanct. Her actions are particularly horrifying because, regardless of claims of love, she discards the responsibility for the survival of her children, a moral principle of parenting recognized in most cultures. The audience might feel pity for Jason and fear of a murderous mother, and Aristotle writes critically because 'no good use is made of the irrationality in Euripides's introduction' of the character of Aegeus into the story which allows Medea to escape (Aristotle 1987: 73, chapter 25). But Euripides is presenting Medea as both a woman and a more-than-human mythic figure. Regardless, Medea's actions have been considered monstrous throughout history because they contravene the basic belief that a mother's love is naturally protective.

If the elaborate costumes, props and sets of Greek theatre suggested imaginative stylization (Green 1994; Wiles 1997), the use of painted fabric masks did not preclude communication of the emotions in performance. The masks presented an expression for a character as we have learned from pottery illustrations and stone copies of theatrical masks found in museum collections (Meineck 2017: 81, 91, 92, images). Peter Meineck discusses the masks of Greek theatre when he draws on neurophysiological research to argue that the mask's ambiguity facilitates the attribution of feeling to faces (2017: 98–9). He argues that an audience member will try to identify and allocate an emotion even when the performer's face is covered and expression limited by a mask.

Contemporary productions of Greek drama often remove classical elements like masks that point to life's uncontrollable aspects and align with Medea's mythic significance. Updated interpretations and adaptations have focused on gender issues as they integrate more recent understandings of parental conflict. In 2000, Deborah Warner directed Fiona Shaw in a production that located the action around a pool, removed Medea's escape and suggested her delusion (Euripides 1994; Dolan 2008: 157–62). Director Carrie Cracknell's *Medea*, adapted by Ben Power for London's National Theatre in 2014, highlighted

Medea's (Helen McCrory) contradictions as she appeared 'rational and irrational', switching from 'the manipulative to the murderous to the unpredictably humane', whereas Jason (Danny Sapani) evaded and rebuffed like a politician (Billington 2014). The dance-like movement of the chorus choreographed by Lucy Guerin for Cracknell's production, however, disrupted its everyday realism (Varney 2017: 176) to imply the vagaries of fate. Rachel Cusk's 2015 version of *Medea* for London's Almeida Theatre, directed by Rupert Goold, was an expressly contemporary domestic drama emphasizing how ex-husband Jason could only see events from his position and could not understand Medea's perspective. As the women around her became condescending, Medea's isolation was further emphasized.

Medea can be interpreted through the concept of motherhood as an institution. Andrea O'Reilly (2010) expands on writer Adrienne Rich's distinction between the reproductive capacity of women and the social institution of motherhood in which women have been accorded limited control. Medea fulfilled social expectation by giving birth and to sons, but she has no control over decisions affecting her family which Jason makes for them all. This distinction in motherhood studies proposes that the historical, patriarchal institution utilizes biology as it restricts women. The framework lends itself to the analysis of the dramatic portrayal of such a fundamental emotional relationship (Komporaly 2006), and it has been applied within an analysis of contemporary drama about the loss of a mother's rights faced with state intervention in families and the removal of children (Hughes 2015). Even if Medea denies the institutional imperative of obedient motherhood and defies its self-sacrificing ideals, it is her rage that comes to the fore and to override her emotional bonds with their children. Euripides's play suggests Medea experiences intense shame as a result of Jason's emotional rejection, and her anger is fuelled by a loss of her social identity as his wife and therefore her social standing. Medea says, 'But stronger than all my afterthoughts is my fury' (Euripides 1967: 96, line 1079).

The larger question remains: how could a parent kill a child or children in filicide? This does happen in extreme instances where the break-up of a marriage and family ends in murder. For example, scenarios in Caryl Churchill's (1994) complex play, *The Skriker*, refer to child death and an underlying violence haunts fragmented family life embodied by a mythic shape-changing figure of vengeance, the Skriker. In *Medea*, anger and shame supplant maternal responsibility, which leads to murderous action and recognizes a contradictory tension between social expectations of feelings and the actual feelings. Ivana Brown (2010) finds that emotional ambivalence is commonly expressed in memoirs about mothering and explains that expectations of 'happiness' can be undermined by 'conflict' and 'anxiety', so that ambivalence 'refers to the coexistence of conflicting and opposing thoughts or feelings' which can be further linked to psychoanalytical ideas such as those about love and hate being at opposite ends of a spectrum, and evident in responses to, and from, children (2010: 121, 122). Medea's revenge is extreme but she and her family are living as exiles in an insecure world (Villalobos 2010), which has consequences for emotional relationships. Euripides does not reveal what Medea's children know about their circumstances. In Medea's world, there are servants and emotional care is separated from the physical care of children. Studies of contemporary parenthood across race and ethnicity expressly point out that social practices determine who undertakes what Arlie Hochschild calls 'emotion work' in society and in the family and in ways that reflect 'feeling rules' in society, and that these continue to be gendered regardless of who does the physical childcare (Garey and Hansen 2011). The emotion work of parenting and the teaching of feeling rules have a central function in family relationships, and in society, and are still largely a female responsibility. Sadly, this manifests in *Medea* through emotional possessiveness over the lives of children.

Hall explains that while Greek tragedy involves suffering and agony, Aristotle considers how art and its poetic distillation can transform horrific events into bearable experience for audiences (2010: 5). Aristotle was particularly concerned with extreme stories about individuals who killed their family members and, by most measures, contravened what most people value, and many in the audience would possibly choose to die themselves rather than commit this deed (Belfiore 1992: 72, 162, note 81). It is the pathos of the story that illuminates Jason's suffering and induces pity or fear (Belfiore 1992: 135). In ancient Greek theatre Aristotle argues, it was not the embodied acting of suffering as happens in later theatre; rather, the 'emotional focal point' lay in the artistic structuring of narrative development, irrespective of the performance, staging and its machinery (Belfiore 1992: 130–1).

The emotionally burdened character might experience a type of madness, and Aristotle gives the example of Oedipus who discovers that, unknowingly, he married his mother and thus he blinds himself (1987: 46, chapter 11). Audience members pity Oedipus and fear such circumstances including the ensuing madness. Should Medea's behaviour be considered a comparable type of madness? While she seems emotionally unbalanced, Medea is also controlled and calculating so that Euripides's play is usually considered a narrative about revenge rather than madness. She admits she can live with the guilt but not the mockery of enemies (1967: 86, line 797). The depiction of insanity in theatre generally involves loss of self-control and excessive emotional display such as in Shakespeare's depictions of madness – for example, in King Lear's scene on the heath in *King Lear* (2009b: 76–9, 3.2). Extreme emotional expression, however, should not be confused with mental illness. In twentieth-century drama, symptoms are attributed to individual pathology and framed more appropriately within psychiatric diagnosis (Harpin and Foster 2014). In realistic drama about mental illness, emotional disturbance happens in relation to medical intervention and clinical diagnosis, and often in an institutional setting.

Dramatic stories model extreme emotional behaviour but this was criticized historically. The ancient Greek word for an actor is 'hypocrite' (*hypokrites*), one who pretends or deceives since theatre involves mimesis or copying. Aristotle addresses criticism from the philosopher Plato (1972) that staging poetic verse is a poor imitation of life and its emotions. In *The Republic of Plato*, Plato explains that life itself is an imitation of pure ideals and he rejects the mimetic function of poetic works that become the emulation of what is already a copy. Plato wants to ban theatre because it discourages restraint and he writes 'to enter into another's feelings must have an effect on our own: the emotions of pity our sympathy has strengthened will not be easy to restrain' and that watching comedy encourages imitation of unsuitable behaviour (1972: 338). As Hans-Thies Lehmann explains, Plato feared that the copying of a character from theatre would destabilize personal self-identity (2016: 24). It is the arousal of extreme emotional feelings by the poetic narrative that is particularly undesirable. A character's bad behaviour could be emulated in society.

Aristotle's ideas seek to redeem theatre through his exploration of learning from the emotional impact and especially where theatrical art improves on the original instance. Hall reiterates that there is a type of pleasure in this process of engaging with intense emotions (2010: 6). Audience members synthesize emotional developments which were not of their own making, while gaining from the example of what happens even to 'good' characters. Aristotle is arguing that theatre needs to be mimetic of processes or rhythms in nature inclusive of humans so that mimesis is broader than mere replication of the stories and emotions of social life (Belfiore 1992: 53).

Historically, then, the idea of an emotion was thought of as joined with the accompanying feeling. As the dramatic action unfolds through the narrative, Aristotle describes how thought and feeling converge in catharsis (*katharsis*) experienced by audience members. Aristotle's idea of catharsis is generally understood as engagement through artistically crafted perceptual 'change' within a build-up of tension in tragedy (and the way in which emotional responses such as fear are also felt bodily) that reaches a peak and then dissipates

(Belfiore 1992: 28). (This was deemed a process of cleansing and purification in line with ancient Greek medical ideas for treating the body.) Catharsis suggests a chain of heightened emotional reactions progressively intensifying until their release or relief, and contained by the duration of the performance and shared by the audience. It is valued by Aristotle for its capacity to provide a type of safety valve because theatre can divert feeling from less controlled circumstances in social life and which Plato feared. Lehmann explains that this Aristotelian notion of emotional purification has been understood to constitute a type of social sublimation. In relation to tragedy, Lehmann writes: 'Pain, suffering, terror, fear, failure and collapse become matters of gestural and linguistic communication' and constitute 'the tragic effect' (2016: 161). Further, Lehmann contends that while catharsis is connected to the expression of suffering, there is a redeeming moment of joy that 'explodes oppressive sensations' (Lehmann 2016: 161). This suggests that theatre allows enjoyment of strong emotions per se, and emotions are revealed to exist either in compatible alignment such as shame and humiliation or as oppositions such as love and hate, joy and fear. A cathartic cycle thus includes the tension that arises from contradictory emotions. In *Medea*, the cathartic cycle extends from understanding Medea's angry indignation at Jason's betrayal of them to the horror that she kills her own children.

The assumptions are that: the theatrical narrative communicates ideas of the emotions, thought stimulates emotional feeling and the intensity that develops through catharsis can have a pleasurable effect for the audience. A cathartic cycle encourages the audience to engage with the motivation and behaviour, and Aristotle advocates selective emotional results that redeem theatre from the criticism of its imitative falsity. Whether cathartic theatre circumvented an eruption in other circumstances such as unrest threatening the social order or not, theatre has historically offered a space in which to temporarily engage with the emotions of extreme events. As Lehmann (2016) explains, however, in early-twentieth-century explorations of such ideas in relation to the struggles of the working class and capitalism, catharsis was considered to forestall emotionally motivated behaviour that might change society because it became contained within theatrical space and such emotional restriction was politically criticized. The longstanding perception is that the emotional experience of theatre might be powerful, but it does not necessarily transfer into beneficial social action.

Shakespeare's comic lovers: Performing the passions

Although a dramatic narrative conveys ideas of the emotions and emotional motivation, language describes how characters feel, their passions, and in lasting ways with, for example, the poetic expression of Shakespeare's drama. Joseph Roach explains that in the seventeenth century, the passions were considered phenomena arising from the body and which theatre confirmed could become unbalanced and needed to be returned to balance (1985: 47). The body was medically treated according to whether there was an equilibrium in its fluids, which consisted of blood, phlegm, black bile and yellow bile. Gail Paster (2004) explains that the physiological and psychological dimensions of the emotions were unified so that emotional disturbance was treated in physical ways, and historical ideas attributed qualities like heat or cold to the phenomena or humours of the body described as sanguine (blood), phlegmatic (phlegm), melancholic (black bile) and choleric (yellow bile). Emotions were believed to constitute natural forces in keeping with the elements of fire, earth, water and wind, and they presented problems in everyday life and excess could lead to death (Paster 2004: 11). But as scholars of Shakespeare's drama point out, advice about the impact of emotions on behaviour was as important as the beliefs about humours and their fluid composition (Meek 2012). From the perspective of seventeenth-century Christian belief and moral instruction for improving behaviour, Thomas Wright links the senses and the emotions and writes that 'most men inordinately follow the unbridled appetite of their sensual passions' but should be guided instead to moderation through Christian example (1620: 15). Wright contends that the body's constitution will become unbalanced unless reason is used to control the passions of the mind (1620: 17).

Historically, acting involved understanding the physical movement of passion and in order to transform the body. Since passion meant to suffer, an actor needed to portray how someone becomes overwhelmed and the power of passion involved a literal display of suffering that would 'act on' others and move them (Roach 1985: 27, 28). Actors in Shakespeare's era could draw on techniques for oration and rhetorical delivery that went back to Aristotle and descriptions of how a speaker could use vocal tone and facial expression to suggest either pleasure or pain in order to persuade listeners. In Shakespeare's *Hamlet*, Hamlet's thinking is presented through rhetorical questions including those of his famous soliloquy about emotional choices early in act three, 'To be, or not to be: that is the question' in which he asks whether it is mentally better to live with the pain of betrayal or suicide, risking death in a direct confrontation. But effective acting in Shakespeare's era favoured restraint as outlined when Hamlet advises the players to act so that in the 'whirlwind of passion, you must acquire and beget a temperance that may give it smoothness' (*Hamlet*, 3.2.5–7). To be credible, the theatrical performance itself should not seem too exaggerated in its delivery.

The depiction of the emotions and especially romantic love contributes to the durability of Shakespeare's drama. *Twelfth Night* is typically grouped with Shakespeare's comedies about 'love', each of which follows a plot that presents obstacles to the romantic union of the featured lovers. In keeping with the expectations of Shakespeare's era, conventional patterns of relationships are overturned before being reinstated at the play's conclusion. In *Twelfth Night*, Viola and her twin brother, Sebastian, are shipwrecked in Illyria and separated, so that each believes the other to be dead. Sebastian is befriended by Antonio and, assisted by the sea captain, Viola dresses in the clothing of a male page to become Cesario and serve at the court of Duke Orsino. Orsino exemplifies the romantic hero with sincerity, kindness and charm and the disguised Viola is soon completely enamoured with him. But he is in love with the Countess Olivia, who is in mourning over the death of her brother, and she rejects Orsino's attention. Olivia's household includes her steward, Malvolio; a relative, the hard-drinking Sir Toby Belch and his friend Sir Andrew Aguecheek, a potential suitor; her companion Maria; and a jester, Feste. Orsino sends Cesario (Viola) to plead with Olivia on his behalf. Olivia receives Cesario (Viola) and falls for the lovely – unbeknown to her – cross-dressed page bringing messages of love from Orsino. In the central comic plot, Belch, Maria and Aguecheek decide to play a trick on the punitive Malvolio for his pompous attitudes and deceive him into believing that Olivia is in love with him. The play's resolution is prompted by the reappearance of Viola's twin: Sebastian marries Olivia, and Orsino marries Viola (and Sir Toby Belch marries Maria).

Shakespeare's characters describe their emotional feelings for others. While there is tacit agreement that words are inadequate for describing feelings, Shakespeare's play starts by probing the question: how does it feel to love someone? The play opens with Orsino's famous line:

> If music be the food of love, play on;
> Give me excess of it … (1.1.1–2)

The lover's poetic statement makes explicit the way that music can match an inexpressible feeling such as romantic longing. If music captures Orsino's feelings and heightens them, sensory sound experience becomes interchangeable with emotional feeling. As well, music communicates an emotional feeling to others. This points to the well-established theatrical convention of utilizing music to communicate an impression of feeling and its use throughout theatre history to induce mood (see especially Section Three).

Bridget Escolme reiterates that the archetypal romantic lover, Orsino, is 'in love with love itself' (2014: 113). The experience of being in love might be painful but there is also enjoyment in the somatic attunement to intense feeling – the experience of theatre might be comparable. Indeed, Escolme argues that Shakespearean drama depicts the excess of passions. She writes that in Shakespeare's time 'their disease-like, troublesome, excessive quality is what makes passions passions – and love is one of them' (2014: 114). Significantly, the emotions that underscored conflict could be 'a political issue', and theatrical narrative allowed the accepted social limits to be overstepped, debated and then reinstated (Escolme 2014: xvii, xxiii).

Since women did not perform in the public theatres of early modern England, female emotions were part of the theatrical pretence. *Twelfth Night*'s all-male cast offset how public displays of even a fully clothed female body would have been considered scandalous within the religious values of the time. Christianity aligned the masculine mind with a higher order and intellectual pursuit, while medical treatises presented the female body as an imperfect version of the human (male) body and associated the womb with hyper-emotionality and hysteria. This gendered division of thought and emotion was longstanding. Therefore, the Christian Puritans also rejected theatre because of its display of passion, and there were religious sermons against its excesses (Escolme 2014: xvii). Theatre was condemned for its presentation of romance and female characters freely describing and expressing emotions. In *Histrio Mastix: The Players Scourge, or, Actor tragaedie*, William Prynne attacked theatre as anti-Christian and 'workes of Satan', calling actors 'wicked' and condemning theatre's 'lewdness' for influencing society (1633: 4, 5, 42). Prynne was particularly against boy actors for playing women and asks: do theatre players not engage the affections of audience members? In Prynne's own words: 'doe (b) they not enrage their lusts, adde fire and fewell to their unchast affections; (c) deprave their minds, corrupt their manners, (d) cauterize their consciences?' (1633: 3).

It was part of an Elizabethan boy actor's training from about ten years of age to learn to sign female identity through the costume, hair and dress – its semiotics – and to perform the accompanying emotional expression and movement of women. Even though early modern sumptuary laws made it a criminal offence to wear the clothing of another gender or class, the liberty of cross-dressing in theatre offered complex scenarios of gender and its performativity. But in *Twelfth Night*'s dramatic narrative, Viola's cross-dressing is temporary and corrected at the end. Jean Howard speculates about what it meant for Elizabethan women to encounter a type of hidden resistance to their gendered lives, including putting their reputations at risk by attending theatre, noting that some of higher social position might have found these portrayals empowering (1994: 77–80). Howard explains, however, that underneath Viola's disguise is someone disparaging of this effect, given that Viola's disguise is pragmatic, for safety in a potentially hostile masculine world. Viola proclaims that she does not want to be a man and is truly a woman in her love for Orsino. Visual gender switches are counterbalanced by verbal declarations of emotional orientation. The play ensures that Viola's love for Orsino is fulfilled in romantic union, and dramatic happiness perpetuates a conventionally gendered pattern.

The ways in which the meaning of the emotions undergoes modification are revealed in the contrast between the early staging of Shakespeare's drama and contemporary interpretation. In particular, events once considered comic may not continue to be seen in this way. In her comprehensive history of *Twelfth Night*'s production history, Elizabeth

Schafer points out that interpretations have shifted in tone from comedy in the early modern theatre to an emphasis on an underlying unhappiness and pathos in the late twentieth century. As views on the emotions revise over time, dramatic depictions adjust accordingly, keeping pace with the increased scope of romantic relationships and social behaviour. Schafer writes that the trend in recent productions has been to envisage the play 'as a comedy about to collapse into tragedy' (2009: 1). The shift happens through changing emotional attitudes as well as with the prominence given to particular characters in a production. This is amply illustrated by Eamon Flack's 2016 production of *Twelfth Night* for Belvoir Street Theatre, Sydney, which moved between comedy and tragedy while presenting visual design and music to impact on the spectator's engagement through sight and sound. I found the augmented sensory effects made the production imaginatively absorbing and these enhanced the solemn moments of pathos with Feste, the amusing sequences of the trick against Malvolio and the comic action of Olivia's dishevelled appearance.

The idea that falling in love might heighten the body's feeling and sensory experience – its affect – and brighten the surroundings and sharpen visual, tactile and aural perception was suggested by the set and costume design for this production. The colours of the sparse set by Michael Hankin were burnished gold and brilliant orange with molten gold effects that contrasted with the cobalt blue and deep green stage floor. Performers entered in white with white faces, as if in a Harlequin show, and gathered around Orsino (Damien Ryan) who wore a deep rich, crimson velvet doublet. The vibrant and sensuous *Twelfth Night* costuming by Stephen Curtis with its shades of green, orange and gold supported the characterization visually. The lushness of the fabrics and textures created what can be called a haptic sensory effect. The idea of 'haptic' refers to how tactile sensations arise with what is seen. Bodily senses may not function separately as is often presumed but instead engage with the surroundings in ways that can overlap and flow together (Cahill 2010). In the example of the Australian production, the look of costume fabrics evoked sensations of touch with Viola (Nikki Shiels) in vibrant green, Maria (Lucia Mastrantone) in olive green and Olivia (Anita Hegh) in a dark green with black velvet. Donatella Barbieri (2017) places the costume at the centre of theatrical ritual, spectacle and genre, the visual impact throughout theatre history. The decorative elements of costume provide an additional way of conveying information about characters and their emotional relationships and status. While Sir Toby (John Howard) wore orange velvet, the white-faced Malvolio (Peter Carroll) was dressed in Puritan black.

As well, *Twelfth Night*, like most of Shakespeare's comedies, uses music to affirm emotional impressions. Flack's production deployed diverse musical styles, from solemn to dynamic, to heighten emotional appeal. Emele Ugavule who acted Antonio also sang in lieu of the actor playing Feste (Keith Robinson), and Ugavule's accomplished singing was poignant. The musical score by Alan John juxtaposed lines from familiar popular songs about love with soulful period music created for Feste's songs. In the play's first act, Viola envisages being a singer at the Duke's court to gain acceptance as an outsider: at the sea coast, Viola declares her plan to assume a gender ambiguous role:

I'll serve this duke.
Thou shalt present me as an eunuch to him –
It may be worth thy pains – for I can sing. (1.2.55–7)

Thus she suggests that her musical abilities will make her gender ambiguity more acceptable.

Contemporary audiences are likely to respond to *Twelfth Night*'s gender ambiguity as well as its multiple types of romantic attraction. In the play, attraction develops through seeing someone, such as when Olivia meets Viola, or is prevented from seeing someone, such as when Orsino cannot visit Olivia. Attraction can arise from the trappings of wealth and status, in the case of Orsino's desire for Olivia. It can also happen without those things and be sparked instead by poetic speech, such as Viola making her master's case to Olivia, or by a letter, such as the one Maria fakes for Malvolio to discover. It can seem unrequited and one-sided, such as Viola's love for Orsino, or mistakenly assumed to be returned, such as in Malvolio's delusion that Olivia loves him. It can be self-sacrificing like Antonio's love for Sebastian. In *Twelfth Night*, only the clown, Feste, is cynical about romance when he proclaims 'many a good hanging prevents a bad marriage' (1.5.16). It is Olivia who asks of sudden feelings of love, 'Even so quickly may one catch the plague?' (1.5.250). She points to an understanding of an emotional feeling as an infectious condition. The precept that emotional feeling can become contagious within a community has featured in twentieth-century studies of the emotions although these have been primarily concerned with the negative consequences, such as when anger spreads in an uncontrollable crowd (Hatfield, Cacioppo and Rapson 1994).

Significantly, *Twelfth Night* depicts seductive romance as inherently theatrical. The scene in which Olivia meets Cesario (Viola) unfolds as a performance in which Olivia receives Viola's scripted speech of love. It imitates the complex emotional dynamics within theatre between spectator and performer as Olivia falls in love with Viola, who is like an actor expressing words she does not feel. When Olivia says that she does not feel love for Orsino, Cesario (Viola) wins over Olivia by explaining that the lover should camp at her gate, sing love poems in the middle of the night – that is, perform for her – then she would pity him. As events unfold, Olivia sends Malvolio to catch Viola and return a ring. The surprised Viola counters that she did not leave a ring with Olivia and says, 'Poor lady, she were better love a dream' (2.2.23). The imaginative fantasy of love is highlighted. Viola tries to tell the Duke that perhaps Olivia might not come to love him but he refuses to listen, claiming that no woman can deny such a passion or hold such strong feelings of love (2.4). The lover cannot hear that he is not loved.

In asking 'What Is This Thing Called Love?', Mary Evans finds ideas of romantic love overshadow more common familial love but change over time in unromantic ways, influenced by culture and its messages about love (2003: 1). A cultural milieu encourages selective types of attraction, evident in shifts in social preferences for a particular physical appearance. Evans explains that it is artists and writers who have been concerned with 'the way in which we construct love ... [t]he highs and lows of love' (2003: 2). She further points out that beliefs about love are pervasive, and more recently compounded by technology, since 'ideologies of love and romance are deeply seductive' (2003: 20). The idea of the lover is socially shaped and artistic characteristics of romantic appeal adjust accordingly.

Thus, social values have influenced the interpretation of character emotions in *Twelfth Night*. In the history of its production, the status of Viola has shifted from a subsidiary function as a singer in the eighteenth century to that of assertive lead character in late-twentieth-century theatre (Schafer 2009: 1). The all-male casts of Shakespeare's theatre may have produced homoerotic undertones in the scenes between the male-to-female cross-dressed Olivia and Cesario. In contemporary productions, the female performer playing Viola cross-dresses as male, and in the context of increased acceptance of same-sex relationships in the late-twentieth century, these interactions with Olivia can be read as expressions of lesbian desire. Antonio's love for Sebastian is now often interpreted as gay (Schafer 2009: 59). The possibility of homosexual meaning remains in the narrative regardless of which gender plays each character although its variation directly confronts how different types of romantic love are socially sanctioned. Emphasizing the queer dynamics and implying that Orsino was a womanizer, Simon Godwin's 2017 production of *Twelfth Night* for London's National Theatre additionally cast female performers as Feste (Doon Mackichan) and Malvolio (renamed in this production as Malvolia) (Tamsin Greig). Godwin's interpretation expanded the possibilities of queer romance with Malvolia as a repressed lesbian in love with an energetic Olivia who was in turn attracted to a cross-dressed Viola.

By comparison, contemporary productions of Shakespeare's plays by Asian theatre companies have purposefully expanded on the humorous potential and comic emotional range and through the addition of stylistic features from other performance traditions. Notably, The Company Theatre of Mumbai, India, offered alternative comic characterizations in its Hindi-language adaptation of *Twelfth Night* as a musical, a popular form in India. Directed by Atul Kumar, it explored the satirical possibilities to the full with a visually colourful aesthetic (reportedly available on Netflix under the Hindi title, *Piya Behrupiya*). This interpretation had Orsino as a slightly chubby, everyday type (making fun of the aesthete romantic hero) and delivered colonial resonances through the period costume of Malvolio's character and the solemnity of expression (Schafer 2013). An interpretation of Shakespearean comedy through highly stylized physical theatre was also apparent in the well-known and widely seen South Korean production of *A Midsummer Night's Dream from the East*. The Yohangza Theatre Company presented twin Pucks and integrated comic characters and bawdy action from Korean traditional performance and folk stories (Yong Li Lan 2013). The interpretation presented exaggerated physical interactions and clowning action to expand on the comic possibilities of the play.

The overall emotional impression of a production can be changed by the emphasis placed on a particular character. The original comedy in *Twelfth Night* arose from the fun made of the self-righteous Malvolio and his delusion that he would appeal romantically to Olivia. Malvolio's expectation of his improved social status instead meets with social shaming, but this may be less humorous to contemporary audiences who might pity him. If the character of Olivia is highlighted, as in many contemporary productions, then the play is about the right to choose whom to marry and

Olivia's rejection of Orsino may have greater significance than that of a woman in mourning or someone who is simply disinterested. The social world of the original production did not presume women's choice in marriage. Olivia chooses an unknown stranger, seemingly a page servant, over a Lord who is her equal in social position and fortune as if she is free to love whomever and is in control. Her choice looks unobtainable until a neat narrative twist gives her a match in Sebastian and implies a happy future. Theatre's capacity to reconfigure the emotional qualities – comic to sad or vice versa – can also alter the implications of what happens. Hence changing the emotional emphasis can change the theatrical meaning.

The actor's paradox: Eighteenth- and nineteenth-century staging

While seventeenth-century acting was influenced by ideas of persuasion and rhetoric in public speech, delivery also needed to be appropriately emotional in tone. Roach summarizes acting in Shakespeare's time as follows: 'What orators and stage players do, then, is to discover the passions of the mind with their bodies – larynx, limbs, torso, and head together – thereby transforming invisible impulse into spectacle and unspoken feeling into eloquence' (1985: 32–3). While performance aligned with notions of oratory and gesture, and performers looked at and faced whoever was being addressed, the physicalized emotions, the 'passions', were central to acting.

By the eighteenth century, there were manuals for actors that prescribed a gesture (and facial and body position) for each emotion. Dene Barnett summarizes key aspects of illustrations in manuals for grief, surprise, terror, anger, contempt, jealousy, aversion, disparagement, shame and welcome, and explains they were presented in upward or downward action (1987: 38). For example, grief involves raised eyes and eyebrows, 'nostrils distended', and a drooping of the shoulders and limbs, and '"weeping, the shedding of tears, are for the stage actor a matter of consideration, of importance, because weeping is a compassionate and serious mood; as against that, crying, howling are ridiculous"' (quoted in Barnett 1987: 38–9). Excessive expression was discouraged. Aspects of surprise involve widening the eyes and mouth, and arms outward, whereas anger involves frowning and nostril flaring, and contempt, turning away with the legs and arms. In addition, characters who were stock types were often defined by particular qualities such as wily deviousness or trusting innocence. For example, in Italian Carlo Goldoni's mid-eighteenth-century comic, *The Servant of Two Masters*, characters try to outsmart others when a servant, Truffaldino, works for two households and Beatrice cross-dresses as her dead brother to claim money owed him; and in Frenchman Guilbert de Pixérécourt's tragic *Coelina, or the Child of Mystery* adapted from a novel in 1800, the innocent, wronged, Coelina and her father are pursued by a villain.

The French philosopher, Denis Diderot, wrote about the emotion of eighteenth-century actors as part of his exploration of existence, arguing that emotional delivery in theatre requires skill and technique as the actor needs to remain consistent from one performance to the next. A performer who waits for inspiration might deliver an effective performance one night but not the following night. Instead, Diderot argues, the actor must think about what happens in life and work to create the illusion of feeling, and this effort should not be apparent to the audience. Diderot believes that a good performer restrains and controls his or her emotional feeling in order to deliver a consistent performance and that this requires both physical and mental discipline. The idea that the actor does not feel what he or she portrays became known as 'Diderot's paradox'.

In relation to philosophical notions of the self, however, an actor's capacity implied that the interior self could be blank (Roach 1985: 136). Diderot frames his ideas in a dialogue and 'The First' voice asks, 'Have you ever thought on the difference between the tears raised by a tragedy of real life and those raised by a touching narrative?' (1957: 20). In real life, Diderot suggests, the feeling and its bodily reactions happen to someone instantly but a theatrical drama must be crafted to build to its emotional impact, and this effect has to be managed through the acting. But Diderot points out that tears and other expressions in life do not necessarily elicit feeling in the way a good actor can through sustained development. Diderot describes English actor David Garrick's facial expression changing from 'delight' to 'tranquillity' to 'surprise' then 'astonishment', 'sorrow', 'horror' and 'despair' and asks, can he 'have experienced all those feelings and played this kind of scale in concert with his face? I don't believe it' (Diderot 1957: 33). Diderot concludes this versatility is the result of acting technique and it shows how theatre can be especially effective in its simulation of emotional feeling.

Diderot's paradox, that accomplished actors do not feel the specific emotion they perform, continues to be confirmed in more recent investigations of the acting of emotion. In a major study, Elly Konijn interviewed hundreds of actors in Europe and the United States and found that actors do not experience the character's emotions as they portray them (2000: 144). Rather, actors 'create the illusion of real emotions' from everyday life (Konijn 2000: 34). In another research project, Eric Hetzler concludes that the actor seeks control and develops a separate awareness of the expressed emotions of the character but this is not personally or bodily felt (2007: 70).

The key concept of restraint in acted emotion may have varied in delivery across theatre history, but it continued to be a point of discussion. Expression had to fulfil audience expectations, as well as conform to the moral values and social propriety of the age. This conformity was typified by nineteenth-century melodrama when a performer had to display character virtue and show remorse for the transgression of social morals (Bell 2007). Melodrama depicted suspenseful emotional extremes of anguish over transgression and often involved adaptations such as Thomas Holcroft's 1802 English translation of Pixérécourt's *Coelina* as *A Tale of Mystery* which he labelled 'Melo-drame'. Nineteenth-century melodrama was dominated by the plot centring on a heroine and a hero, and a heinous villain who placed the characters in extreme circumstances and emotional distress to suit his purpose, but when the villain was duly exposed, the moral order and its pleasant emotions were reinstated. Melodrama developed into sensationalist theatre with, for example, the play adapted from Mary Elizabeth Braddon's 1862 novel, *Lady Audley's Secret*, about a female villain who commits murder to maintain her second bigamist marriage to an aristocrat. Sensationalist theatre was suspenseful and capable of inducing bodily sensations and reactions such as holding the breath and tensing the muscles.

By the late nineteenth century, however, naturalistic theatre emerged to replicate the social world in realistic detail. This naturalism required innovation in acting practice and it did not acknowledge the audience, creating what has come to be called 'the fourth wall'. Although notions of emotional psychology were not widespread until the 1870s, when publications such as Alexander Bain's (1868) *Mental and Moral Science*, began to appear, readers and theatre audiences comprehended the importance of human emotion within relationships and within the organization of society as well as the purpose of marriage in the maintenance of the prevailing social order. But the stage was depicting the conditions of real life for the first time and exposing social problems in domestic settings, as it rejected the moral 'simplicities of melodrama' and the idealism of 'romantic poetic drama' (Sprinchorn 2007: 1124). Now under the guidance of the director, naturalistic theatre evolved into realist theatre, which removed the superficial replication of the social world in the visual staging while remaining socially truthful in the play's content. Realist drama, then, continued to require distinctive approaches to the performance of emotion.

At the same time a performer on the realist stage needed to embody concepts of what is believed about the psychology of emotional feeling. The selection and imitation of the emotions undergo considerable change in the history of theatre, and this is particularly apparent through a gradual expansion of the range of social identities and emotional experiences presented on the twentieth-century stage.

Stanislavski's Emotion Memory and realist theatre

New ways of acting emotions were integral to the progressive development of realist theatre in which characters describe emotional and other subjective feelings. Henrik Ibsen's and Anton Chekhov's realistic dramas prompted psychological interpretations, and theatre artists grappled with how to act the characters in socially believable ways. The increasing importance accorded emotional feeling in the field of psychology did influence theatre and acting during a pivotal period of change within early-twentieth-century realism. Emotional expression had to appear lifelike to audiences, and this meant being less theatrically demonstrative and more subdued in comparison with previous styles of gestural acting including those of nineteenth-century melodrama. André Antoine in France in the 1890s and Constantin Stanislavski in Russia in the 1900s were the first creators of new methods for 'natural' acting (Tait 2018). As styles of delivery continued to evolve, the approach to acting emotions would become a source of major disagreement.

Stanislavski pioneered a distinctive approach to acting in 1898 from his work directing Chekhov's play *The Seagull* for the Moscow Art Theatre (MAT). This play about theatre, writing and acting was an important landmark in the history of theatre because Stanislavski rehearsed at length and encouraged actors in role to express emotion as if there was no audience. (Stanislavski would continue to experiment with the acting of emotions throughout his working life.) Actor Vasily Toporkov recalled his first impressions of Stanislavski's subsequent MAT production of Chekhov's *The Cherry Orchard*, '"But those are not actors! They are real people"' (1998: 34). Toporkov would later work with the MAT where Stanislavski advised the actor to remove all thoughts about 'your own emotional experiences and feelings' and focus on what would preoccupy the character in the moment (Toporkov 1998: 54).

Stanislavski (2010) would write books on actor training that became known as 'the System', and his techniques were influential globally (Pitches and Aquilina 2017). *An Actor Prepares* (published in English in 1936) and *Building a Character* (published in 1949) contain techniques and exercises while the earlier Stanislavski's *My Life in Art* (published in English in 1924 and in Russian in 1926) presented the director's key principles. *An Actor Prepares* set out Stanislavski's (2010) ideas in a fictionalized process of directing, expressed through the words of a director, Tortsov, as he teaches student actor, Kostya Nazanov, how to act. Tortsov points out that regardless of what an actor believes is happening, the acted emotional expression needs to be convincing. He advises the actor must work with 'imagination, concentration, objects, logic and sequence, Bits and Tasks, wants, effort and actions, truth, belief, Emotion Memory, communication, Adaptations and other Elements' (Stanislavski 2010: 285).

The chapter on Emotion Memory outlines how an actor adapts a personal emotional response to that of the character. The actor needs to remember an event in life and its accompanying emotions by first recalling aspects of sense experience. The memory of the sensory and the emotional experience then informs the characterization. Significantly, Stanislavski rejected the idea of directly focusing on emotional and other feelings in acting because this was too difficult (Tait 2002: 93–4; Neuerburg-Denzer 2014: 79). The way in which remembered emotional feeling intersects with, for example, the interpretation of intention and belief is important for communication in theatre. A performer should work with an emotionally inflected intention for the character summarized by what he or she wants from the situation. To some extent, emotional expression becomes dependent on the integration of thought and imagination (Morton 2013), and connected to the other elements of acting (Kemp 2012). An idea of an emotion can determine how intention is acted, and in strategies that use verbs for intention with the emotions expressed as adverbs. For example, if a character's action for a scene is summarized with the verb 'to talk' with another character, its delivery can be enhanced by adding and expressing one or more of the following emotions such as with 'sympathy, love, pity, compassion', or 'hate, avenge, torment', according to the identity of the characters and the dramatic circumstances (Stanislavski 2010: 671).

As well as outlining broad principles, Stanislavski's System provides practical strategies and divides a play into sections allocating an action or objective for the character in each section that can be either physical or a silent intention such as 'to persuade' another character. A performer creates an overall objective, a 'through line of action', for the character in the play such as 'to deceive'. Nonverbal acting for intensification or an emotional contradiction underlies what is being delivered in the spoken text and to create a subtext. Stanislavski clearly set out an approach to acting emotions that rejected waiting for emotional inspiration during performance and advocated prolonged and careful preparation in rehearsal. Felt experience happens continuously but the acting of emotions needs to be selective (Stanislavski 2010: 196). He gives the example of Shakespeare's Hamlet, who attacks his uncle, the King, with a sword towards the end of *Hamlet*, and if the actor relies on being inspired in the moment of performance, Stanislavski suggests, he may well injure the other actor (Stanislavski

2010: 208). The actor must be in control. Stanislavski writes, 'We aren't masters of spur-of the-moment experiences, they master us [...] if spontaneous feelings do arise, then let them appear when they are needed' (2010: 208). He implies that spontaneous feelings can be explored in the rehearsal and because, he continues, it is unusual to have suitable types of feeling for the first time while performing on the stage, it is important to rehearse with emotional emphasis beforehand.

Stanislavski was influenced directly by Théodule Ribot in France and his work on the psychology of emotions, and indirectly by Charles Darwin and American philosopher William James writing on emotions (Whyman 2008: 4). A distinction between the emotions and emotional feelings had, by the turn of the twentieth century, emerged in such work, and James's theory reversing the previous order so that thought followed bodily feeling would become particularly influential. James (1984) suggests that the emotional feelings were the dominant experience so that physiological reactions inside the body take precedence. This emphasis on the primacy of the physiology of the body's feelings would be subsequently disputed in studies of emotion by researchers such as Richard Lazarus (1994) and Nico Frijda (1994) in psychology arguing that orientation to the world and appraisal of external stimulus remain crucial to how a feeling develops. The acting of emotions was being explored at a pivotal period of theatre history with the advent of early realist drama such as *The Seagull*, and at a time when there were important developments in psychology among theorists of human (and animal) emotions.

The main characters in Chekhov's *The Seagull* include two female actors and two male writers, who describe their subjective feelings – demanding then, interpretation in acting. Chekhov's characters frequently describe their feelings using quotes from theatre and literature, which suggest a common practice. Nina, the younger actor, is starting out as the play begins, and by the end, she is experienced in theatre and in romantic relationships although disappointed by both. She declares that she must persevere with acting. Nina explains:

'I'm a real actress. I enjoy acting. I adore it. I get madly excited on stage, I feel I'm beautiful' (Chekhov 1991: 114). In this confession, Nina encapsulates the appeal of acting as similar to the emotional feeling of a love affair. This doubling of the character as performer draws attention to emotions in performance. Nina also explains about her younger self, 'what emotions we felt – like exquisite, delicate blossoms' (Chekhov 1991: 114). She remembers youthful emotions as intensely pleasurable in comparison with the emotions of the present; this may reflect the function of how emotional feelings are remembered. By the end of *The Seagull*, Nina is unable to shed her personal emotional difficulties and these contribute to her dissatisfaction with her acting: a love of performing does not overcome her self-doubt.

In order to direct *The Seagull* and to clarify emotional interactions in this new form, Stanislavski wrote a novel-like commentary to accompany the play, describing every physical move on stage and each emotional interaction between the characters in considerable detail. For example, in a scene towards the play's end, Treplev is a successful playwright but knows that Nina cannot love him: a single stage direction has Treplev tear up his manuscript. Under Stanislavski's direction Treplev watched Nina depart, dropped his glass, and then burned his manuscripts and letters before he exited. Stanislavski tries to convey the impression of Treplev's subjective feeling as he outlines that Treplev 'falls into a reverie again' and 'rubs his forehead disconsolately' (Stanislavsky 1952: 283). Offstage he shoots himself in an action that reflects existential hopelessness and despair, as well as providing an early dramatic depiction of clinical depression leading to suicide. The process of acting a character's felt experience – that is, externalizing inner turmoil – remains particularly challenging for performers. It requires the performance of emotional feeling to appear as if it were being subjectively experienced. To appear lifelike in Stanislavski's approach to acting, then, the performer often appears to suppress emotional feeling (as happens in life) rather than demonstratively express it (as happens in theatre).

Stanislavski's 'System' underwent several changes over his career as he searched for the best way to act while appearing not to act. As Sharon Carnicke reveals, regardless of the form, Stanislavski highlighted 'experiencing' in acting, although this becomes reduced to 'feeling' in the English translation (2009: 130–1). In Stanislavski's theoretical and practical use of the concept of 'experiencing', an actor is fully rehearsed so that he or she can be alert and focused on the surrounding stage in the immediate moment and self-aware which enlivens the performance, and Carnicke finds that it indicates how '"flow" often induces a sensation of watching oneself' (2009: 134–5). Flow denotes an awareness of being involved in an experience as it is unfolding but differentiated from that of an emotional feeling as such. Moreover, an actor might not cry tears but the audience will nonetheless (Toporkov 1998: 53–4). (Tears are an involuntary reaction to feelings and commonly associated with feelings of grief. The reader might think of an actor who has elicited tears without shedding tears.) The MAT actor Olga Knipper (Chekhov's wife) who first played Chekhov's major female characters mastered the technique of restraining physical mannerisms and outward signs to draw attention to what seems to be the character's inner experience (Tait 2002: 128).

By the 1920s, Stanislavski had expanded his earlier approach and taken the emphasis off the prior interpretation of emotions and Emotional Memory early in rehearsal. Instead, he now theorized, an actor should first develop physical movement for the character through training outlined in 'Making the Body Expressive' in *Building a Character* (Stanislavski 2010: 355–64). To set the preconditions for experiencing the performance as it happens, Stanislavski developed what he called 'active analysis' where the performer works actively and physically from the outset in rehearsal and internal motivation emerges out of the foundational physical action. This interpretation of the System is widely used today through the teaching legacy of one of his students, Maria Knebel, who preserved Stanislavski's later understanding that acting should be 'psychophysical', combining inner purpose with the physical movement of the body and developed through the use of improvisation early in rehearsal (Carnicke 2009: 190–1; Merlin 2003: 18). The term 'psychophysical' describes the predominant approach in Western actor training.

The results of Stanislavski's investigations are acknowledged in the wider cultural study of the emotions. For example, the influential social researcher Arlie Hochschild (1983) refers to Stanislavski on emotional depth in her own concept of 'emotion work', although acting subjective emotional feeling should not be considered the same as feeling it in life. What Hochschild terms the 'emotion labor' expected of smiling, cheerful workers in service industries might also be applicable to the reproduction of emotions in theatrical and other performance mediums (Solga 2019). This is an idea of selective emotional expression as part of labour – that is, the performance of emotions in the workplace and in society. It remains relevant to theatrical performance ranging from the managed consumption of emotion in commercial theatre to that of sublimated feeling in interactive performance (see Section Three). Importantly, then, Stanislavski was influenced by, and in turn contributed to, the study of emotion in society. In his extensive critique of emotion and what are termed 'higher order' or 'cultural' emotions shaped by social interactions (in contrast to a disputed category of basic physiological ones), Robert Roberts refers to Stanislavski's writings to confirm how emotions are cognitively accessed in order to be reproduced in credible ways to others. Roberts draws on Stanislavski to argue that there are emotional feelings that are neither pretence nor unconscious but exist somewhere in between (2003: 33–4). Performance creates its own category of emotional experience.

Stanislavski encouraged innovative lifelike acting by an ensemble of actors through his own direction of early realist drama and influenced the formulation of cause-and-effect cognitive explanations for emotions in twentieth-century theatre. There are explicit and implicit legacies of Stanislavski's approach to acting emotions throughout twentieth-century theatrical and cinematic practices as well as in social ideas. Significantly, the doing of action associated with his later approach has proven adaptable to the shift from fully rounded character psychology in realist texts to partial impressions of a persona in less realist texts such as in Robert Lepage's *Needles and Opium* (see Section Two). Stanislavski is associated with realism even though he worked with non realistic forms such as symbolism and opera and experimented with form throughout his working life. The effort to communicate emotions that seem believable in contemporary contexts continues to require sustained experimentation of the kind Stanislavski considered necessary.

Controversial psychologies in Method Acting

By the late twentieth century, psychophysical approaches combining physical movement and the interpretation of psychological experiences and attitudes typified Western actor training (Merlin 2003: 155–6), although the balance between the two differs widely. Stanislavski's early Emotion Memory is emphasized in its application in what became known as 'Method Acting' with its psychological emphasis that strongly encouraged an actor's personal recall. Method Acting has been controversial because adherence to this type of technique created challenges for younger actors whose personal experience could not match that of a complex role, and the concern that introspection inhibited emotional delivery. Yet in many respects, film and other screen acting needed Method Acting to create a psychological performance suited to camera close-ups. An actor's communication of a character's subjective experience involves the face and eyes and often without speech. On screen, small facial movements are used to suggest inner feeling.

The Method and its parent, Stanislavski's System, are what the words suggest, and they involve studying what happens in social worlds: developing a purpose or an objective; improvising to find the best approach; appearing to talk with other characters; and finding appropriate emotions in a corresponding personal example. Their shared premise is that if performers follow principles and procedures and engage in exercises, techniques and strategies over time, they will develop a body of skills which can make them competent actors. Method Acting became widely associated with Lee Strasberg, who was inspired by seeing Stanislavski's direction of MAT productions in New York on tour with Chekhov's *The Cherry Orchard* and Maxim Gorky's *The Lower Depths* in 1923 and 1924. Strasberg became the dominant figure associated with Method Acting over thirty-five years of his teaching in New York at the Actors Studio, encouraging an actor to calibrate personal experience in rehearsal for emotional interpretation in performance. He later opened a comparable institute in Los Angeles which points to Strasberg's influence on actors who became successful in Hollywood cinema. For example, Geraldine Page acknowledges how Strasberg's teaching helped her act demanding roles and to remove distracting mannerisms (Malague 2012: 54–5, 48). But there were other important approaches to acting that emerged from the Stanislavski-inspired Group Theatre during the 1930s, after MAT actors, Richard Boleslavski and Maria Ouspenskaia, emigrated to New York and taught Stanislavski's earlier approach and Emotion Memory in which the actor finds an equivalent experience (Vineberg 1991: 5). A contemporary of Strasberg and member of the Group Theatre, Stella Adler was an equally influential teacher of actors in New York and Adler taught Marlon Brando who was considered the iconic Method actor and often associated with Strasberg (Malague 2012: 58, 106).

Adler and Strasberg disagreed about actor training and Adler travelled to work with Stanislavski in Paris for five weeks in 1934 and, returning to the United States, followed Stanislavski's later emphasis on physical action over psychological impetus, and taught that emotions should be those of the character. Adler stresses the use of thought and '"imagination"' and '"given circumstances"' to interpret the emotions of characters in careful script analysis which is indicative of Stanislavski's ongoing requirement (Malague 2012: 82). Put simply, actors contextualize external action and develop the internal responses of a character in relation to the social circumstances in the text.

In a different approach again, Group Theatre member Sanford Meisner stressed the actor's responsiveness in the immediate moment of the performance using repetition in training to develop this capacity. Meisner was also influenced by Euvgeny Vakhtangov, who had worked with Stanislavski but differed by pursuing the belief that the actor should remain focused in the immediate present. Thus Meisner's interactive process for 'emotional aliveness' relied on the literal doing of an action and working directly with another actor in detailed ways (1987: 24, 78). His work specifically encouraged an 'actor's behaviour and "reactions" in performance' instead of internalized motivation (Stinespring 2000: 98). This is still a trained skill but one that downplays the inner psychology of the role.

As Steve Vineberg (1991) explains, however, twentieth-century Method Acting produced an expectation for what is often called 'genuine' or 'authentic' emotion. Yet this labelling can be misleading since the emotions do not have fixed qualities and acting styles for expressing emotions needed to change over time to interpret new types of drama and thus remain credible to the audience of the day. The issue of whether an actor should focus on his or her personal emotional memory remains contested. Marc Gordon points out that Strasberg's approach rehearses and follows Stanislavski's ideas of not becoming overwhelmed by emotional feeling in performance, emphasizing remembered experience through the sight, sound, taste and touch – that is, drawing on sensory experience to evoke emotions (2000: 53). The actor trains his or her sensory body in conjunction with emotions. Strasberg's process has been a major influence on the performance of emotion in film through the work of many of the best-known twentieth-century cinema actors (Marlon Brando, Al Pacino, Marilyn Monroe, Ellen Burstyn, Jack Nicholson, Paul Newman, Joanne Woodward and Dustin Hoffman, among them) who were regular participants in his weekly classes.

It is Strasberg's approach to teaching that has been particularly criticized because of the power imbalance between teacher and student that created an additional emotional dynamic in training and rehearsal. Rosemary Malague finds that this imbalance of 'emotion control' was most often felt by female actors; she writes, 'Strasberg's paternalistic teaching style is filled with gender biases (whether he intended them or not)' in the selection of roles and advice on how to act them (2012: 33). While Strasberg's teaching style seemed authoritarian in accounts given by actors of how he chastised them including hitting a female performer (Malague 2012: 52), his teaching was valued for detailed work with professional film actors in which the performers delivered a scene for his feedback. The personal judgement of the teacher and/or director who singularly decided whether a performance worked and whether the emotion was convincing, often resembled psychotherapy. A famous example of this teaching involves Marilyn Monroe who, as an established film actor, took classes with Strasberg, and the teaching and personal lives became fused when actor Paula Strasberg, Lee's wife, became Monroe's personal coach travelling with her (Malague 2012: 62–71). One particular risk is that a conventionally gendered director–performer dynamic (male director, female actor) will validate stereotypical emotional expression in performance.

The legacy of the 'psychophysical' approach remains commonplace in training actors in emotional expression and 'physical embodiment' in their preparations for a role

(Merlin 2003: 134) and has been influential in countries other than Russia and the United States. Practised in China from the late 1930s, Stanislavski's System became officially sanctioned in 1949 and was subsequently guided by Russian experts (Liu 2017: 150). Siyuan Liu describes an application by director, Jiao Juyin, who worked with both Chinese traditional theatre practices and Western play production by combining the performer's mental imagery and depictions of interiority developed through physical training. As Stanislavski's System spread globally, it mixed with longstanding national/cultural traditions leading to innovative convergence and sometimes resistance as happened on the Indian subcontinent at times. Syed Jamil Ahmed (2017) discusses a hybrid acting approach that developed in Bangladesh's modern theatre to create a more emotional delivery for new plays and productions of Western classics such as Ibsen's *A Doll's House*; it was performed by postgraduate theatre students who were encouraged to undertake self-exploration to develop their roles. Ahmed finds an interculturally shaped practice emerges from these productions in which the emotions are 'articulated by means of the face (primary) and hands (secondary) in a way that strikes the "right" balance between "art" and "life"' in 'simplified realism' that is not melodramatic, and relies on conviction and vocal technique in the separation of the 'I' of the actor and 'not-I' of the character (Ahmed 2017: 420).

In the twenty-first century, numerous theatre practitioners seek to learn both Western and Eastern approaches through specialist workshops. Intensive training to master Eastern theatre techniques for Western actors can enhance approaches to emotional expression and, in addition, question the automatic application of a Western-derived psychological explanation. Phillip Zarrilli (2009) integrates intensive physical training from southern India into his approach, utilizing the traditional *kathakali* physical performance. He explains: 'The actor's breath animates not only the particular facial expression to which the audience's attention is drawn, but simultaneously enlivens and activates the actor's entire body as it assumes a dynamic posture appropriate to the particular emotional state' (Zarrilli 2009: 35). The *kathakali* tradition has set facial expressions for emotions, such as love, amusement, pathos, fear, fury, repulsion, wonder and peace, and often associated with a particular identity (Zarrilli 2009: 36). The predetermined facial expression and embodied pose communicate a specific emotion to audiences.

While this might seem similar to stylized eighteenth-century European manuals for acting, it is more compatible with Bertolt Brecht's ideas of demonstrating a character's social and class position with an accompanying emotion. Brecht's artistic collaborations created important political drama and he rejected Stanislavski-influenced approaches for political reasons, arguing in his theoretical writing that theatre needs to both entertain and educate its audiences and to encourage them to think rather than emotionally feel. Emotion in theatre should be recognizable for its social significance.

Brecht's separations: Theatre for a scientific age

One of the most influential twentieth-century theorists of theatre, Bertolt Brecht was born in 1898 in Germany, served towards the end of the First World War and, fleeing Hitler's Germany, he returned to East Germany after the Second World War to create the Berliner Ensemble and died in 1956 in East Berlin. The political turmoil in early-twentieth-century Germany exposed Brecht to socialist strategies to combat poverty in the aftermath of war, and Marxist ideas about how society should be structurally changed to benefit the working classes, and theatre was considered a useful public platform for such ideas (Mumford 2009). Brecht argues that theatre should make spectators think rather than emotionally feel in order to foster understanding that leads to political action. But Brecht's approach includes thinking about the emotions. This aligns with philosophical ideas of how emotion can be evaluated – that is, emotion is thought – going back to Aristotle, who writes that after plot and dramatic action, 'the third property of tragedy is thought' (Aristotle 1987: 40, chapter 6).

Brecht separates emotion and thought as he distinguishes what he calls epic theatre from the prevalent realist dramatic theatre (Brecht 1987: 37–8). He contrasts how dramatic theatre's evocation of sensations and feelings is immersive and brings the spectator close in passive ways, whereas epic theatre reveals social truth so as to make the spectator observant and questioning in ways that encourage decision-making and action. Brecht rejects the acting of emotional feeling that appears to be happening to the character in the present moment because it absorbs the spectator's attention. The assumption is that feeling usurps thought. But Brecht's epic theatre is not so much anti-emotion as it is against how emotion is seamlessly delivered in realist theatre and discouraged thought about the social circumstances of the characters. For Brecht, the very effectiveness of the lifelike acting of emotions is its flaw. In line with modernist thinking that social progression would result from the rational application of objective scientific knowledge, Brecht's theory reflects the separation of cognition and emotion in twentieth-century scientific discourse.

A crucial opposition for Brecht is the 'reason' of epic theatre and 'feeling' in dramatic theatre, and he looks to stage 'reason' in a sequence of attributes that the spectator could observe (1987: 37). He advocates 'a radical *separation of the elements*' of theatrical production rather than fusing them, which he says induces 'hypnosis', 'intoxication' or a 'fog' in the spectator (Brecht 1987: 37–8, italics in the original). Brecht rejects the way an actor merges with a character and advocates instead reminding audiences that they are watching a performance with interruptions to the narrative and characterization. To this end, his practice deploys an exaggeration of theatrical techniques such as narrative interruptions via music and song, and having a performer speak of the character in the third person and announce stage directions.

Brecht developed a concept of *Verfremdungs* (most often translated as estrangement) in theatre that reflected Karl Marx's theory that workers in the capitalist system were alienated from the economic results of their labour. Marx explains that while the labour of workers turns the materiality of nature into objects, they receive only a fraction of the monetary value and this process of capitalist production also creates the '*human commodity*' as a '*mentally* and physically *dehumanized* being' (1975: 336, italics in original). Brecht's concept of *Verfremdungs* was intended as a pedagogical tool. In contrast to other approaches to acting in twentieth-century Western theatre, Brecht praises the distancing evident in traditional Chinese acting when the performer speaks as if quoting the character and creates a highly visual transformation. Brecht argues that an actor in Western theatre should externally sign an emotion rather than act subjective experience. For Brecht, a particular emotion or set of emotions could be signalled with a word or an action that might reveal social hierarchies through what he terms the vocal and/or physical *gestus*. Brecht explains *gestus* as the 'social gest' to reveal the 'mimetic and gestural expression of the social relationships' and by which a performer demonstrates a critical perspective of the character and includes the 'outward expression for [her] his character's emotions, preferably some action that gives away what is going on inside [her] him' (1987: 139). The theatrical staging and music, Brecht argues, 'communicates', explains or ignores the text but at the same time relays an attitude to what is happening (Brecht 1987: 38). This approach allows for cognitive evaluation even as it undermines the belief that the individual's emotional experience is naturally innate and autonomous, and separate from social influence.

Brecht argues that pity or empathy as emotionally felt responses for a character and the character's psychology must be avoided (1987: 136; Cummings 2016: 28). The emotional content of the narrative would be depicted through outward action to produce what Brecht considers to be 'a different class of emotion' (1987: 140). This rejection of pity in Brechtian theatre in order to foster an objective viewpoint happens within an unfolding dynamic that also resists a logical progression and resolution. The Marxist concept of dialectic materialism, in which the tension between opposing classes generates change in society, matches Brecht's extensive deployment of contradiction in theatre and underlies Brechtian drama's unpredictable and perverse qualities. Brecht claims that society follows scientific 'laws of motion' with 'social situations as processes' in which there is always constant change and which theatre should capture (1987: 193). Lara Stevens explains that through his idea of 'dialectic theatre' and its humour, Brecht encourages spectators to critically evaluate the 'zigzag' composition of social history and realize it does not follow a linear progression (2016: 27–8).

Above all, Brecht sought to create a theatre for a scientific age that could reveal how hierarchical economic and political structures shape people's lives and that by distancing theatrical elements including emotional expression, the structural forces that determine the circumstances of the characters could be exposed and scrutinized. Emotions, Brecht insists, should not be hidden behind the illusion of the fourth wall created in conventional realist theatre. In his dialectic theatre, emotional responses need not match those of the characters so 'on seeing worry the spectator may feel a sensation of joy; on seeing anger, one of disgust' (Brecht 1987: 94). In effect, a Brechtian approach in theatre exaggerates the contradictions and oppositions that are inherent in how emotional experience unfolds.

Brecht's political emotions: *The Caucasian Chalk Circle*

Brecht's idea of separation emphasizes emotion that originates in social circumstances, and his drama contradicts the widespread belief that emotional feeling is naturally intrinsic to an individual. While the notion that the experience of emotions is shaped by culture became important in scholarly work of the 1980s (see, for example, Lutz and Abu-Lughod 1990), this idea had already been consciously deployed by Brecht in both his theory and his plays. *The Caucasian Chalk Circle*, written in 1943–4, suggests that emotion is socially acquired as it challenges the belief that caring emotions are biologically innate through a narrative about a female character's heroic efforts to protect a vulnerable baby although she is not the child's biological mother. This example might be contrasted with Medea's negation of her biological bond with her children (discussed earlier in this section).

The emotions and relationships in Brecht's drama are framed within socio-historical circumstances that are brutal. *The Caucasian Chalk Circle*, his collaboration with Danish actor and director Ruth Berlau, is set during a war. Although this story about the conflict between two women over who is the rightful mother of a child parallels a story from the Christian Bible about a dispute resolved with a threat to halve the child (I Kings 3. 16–28), Brecht's play drew on *The Chalk Circle*, a Chinese drama written during the thirteenth-century Yuan dynasty and credited to Li Qianfu, and translated into German and performed in 1925 (Brecht 1987: vi). Poetic verse is interspersed with dramatic dialogue in *The Chalk Circle*, telling the story of the poor Chinese family Ch'ang, surviving on the earnings of the beautiful daughter, Hai-T'ang, who sings and dances – and possibly prostitutes herself – as a 'flower of the Weeping Willow Tree' (Li 1960: 254). A suitor, Ma Chun-Shing, decides to make her his second wife, and five years pass as their son is raised by the first wife, Mrs Ma. Hai-T'ang's impoverished brother returns and Mrs Ma deceives him as she persuades an admirer to help her poison her husband and blame Hai-T'ang, falsely accusing her of having a lover. Fortuitously, Hai-T'ang's brother rescues her and she pleads her innocence before a morally upright magistrate, Pao-Ch'ing. As both women claim to be the mother, the magistrate in the court requests a piece of chalk, saying: 'You will trace below the bench a circle, in the center of which you will place the young child. Then you will order the two women to wait, each of them at opposite sides of the circle' before rushing forward to grab hold of him in a tug-of-war contest (Li 1960: 255). Hai-T'ang does not move and this happens twice, and by refusing to bodily grab him from the circle, she indicates the concern of a true mother for the boy's physical wellbeing. Finally, Mrs Ma is exposed as a criminal, and Hai-T'ang and her son are reunited and inherit the family wealth. Interestingly, Hai-T'ang's immoral past is not judged in this play about how a biological mother's love is true. In conjunction with the play's formal modes of address, the characters tell other characters (and the audience) that they feel sad or angry or humiliated.

Brecht's *The Caucasian Chalk Circle* is relocated to the Russian Caucasus, possibly Georgia, and the historical drama is framed by an extended prologue set in the mid-twentieth-century communist world. In Brecht's adaptation, the Governor's household flees under military attack, while a servant, Grusha, stays behind with the Governor's baby son, Michael, who the Governor's wife, the biological mother, has accidently left behind in the panic. Grusha escapes to the country carrying Michael and reluctantly leaving Simon, a soldier, whom she promises to marry. Grusha becomes emotionally bonded to Michael in their adversity as they journey through the countryside surviving numerous escapades and life-threatening situations. The courtroom scene that replays Li's drawing of the chalk circle has the judge, Azdak, an opportunistic but likeable rogue, say slyly: 'The true mother is she who has the strength to pull the child out of the circle, towards herself' (Brecht 1986: 94). He is being duplicitous. In the context of a law that recognizes the primacy of biology, Grusha might not be the mother, but her ongoing parental care makes her into the mother. Twice Grusha does not move from the edge of the circle. When Azdak asks why she did not pull, she says, 'I've bought him up. Am I to tear him to pieces?' (Brecht 1986: 95). This narrative about the physical test of maternal love echoes across time as *The Caucasian Chalk Circle* overturns the expectation that love is forged only by biology.

The earlier Chinese play assumes that biological connections are irreversible, whereas *The Caucasian Chalk Circle* conveys them as unreliable. Its characters behave in a self-serving and cowardly manner within the struggle for survival. Even Grusha marries a supposedly dying man for money, an arrangement negotiated by his mother, although he suddenly recovers when the war is over, his ill health revealed as a ploy to escape becoming a soldier. The wider context suggests that Grusha is also self-interested when the Singer describes how she took Michael 'like booty', 'like a thief' (Brecht 1986: 25). But this accusation is not altogether convincing since Grusha risks her life at several points in the narrative and takes moral responsibility. It does suggest that Grusha is surprised by the relationship. Similarly the attachment between Grusha and Simon might initially seem pragmatic rather than romantic, but the play depicts it as emotionally durable, and both are in despair when they are finally reunited, and Grusha has married someone else to aid Michael's survival. Azdak authorizes a divorce for a price, and Grusha tells Simon that she took Michael on Easter Sunday when they got engaged so he is a 'child of love' (Brecht 1986: 96). It is not the biological mother who triumphs in this play but Grusha, who loves Michael – and Simon.

Within the chaotic circumstances of social breakdown and war, emotional bonds are central to a child's survival, but the emotional reactions surrounding Michael are fraught with selfish purpose and deception. There is no compassion shown to the baby; for example, a farmer demands an exorbitant fee for milk. Grusha risks her life crossing a dangerous bridge to reach her brother's house, but his wife is unhappy about Grusha and the baby staying there. Even emotional obligations based on family relationships are shown as weak. The emotional indifference of the characters to others arises in a troubled world and Brecht's depictions resist preconceived ideals of the goodness of humanity and reject theatre that validates such moral platitudes.

A mother's attachment to her children is a theme in several of Brecht's major plays including *The Good Person of Szechwan* (written in 1941) and *Mother Courage and Her Children* (written in 1938–9). Like *The Caucasian Chalk Circle, Mother Courage* is also set in war but in this play the mother is unable to save her children in the end, at least in part because she makes a living from following the armies. The plays show the biological mother to be responsible, if not in an idealized way.

Mothering might be ubiquitous across the animal world, but the balance between caregiving due to natural biology and learning from social nurturing varies even for animals. Psychologist Paul Ekman, who argues for basic emotions and pioneered concepts of feeling rules, considers 'all emotions to be basic in the sense that evolution played a role in shaping both the features unique to each emotion, the features emotions share, and their functions', but other researchers have argued the opposite that 'emotions are not givens' determined by biology but changeable 'interpretive ideas' (Ekman and Davidson 1994b: 46–7). Thus biological capacities can be interrupted or circumvented by social conditions. *The Caucasian Chalk Circle* might nonetheless suggest that a woman is hardwired to care for a baby. But even this explanation is countered if a generic maternal function is aligned with the preservation of life. Sara Ruddick's (2009) concept of maternal thinking, for example, imputes that mothering (as a verb) need not be carried out by a biological mother (as a noun). Because mothering involves care and thought, it facilitates cooperation that should be extended more broadly into social values. Importantly, the work of parenting can be gender neutral. Ruddick connects this with nonviolent capacities and striving for peace, although parenting remains identifiable with women because they are largely still socially responsible for the care of others and particularly dependents, young, old and those with a disability, in the '"*rationality of care*"' (2009: 305, italics in original). For this reason, Ruddick argues, it is important to separate the reproductive identity of the female from the work of caring. Grusha's behaviour in *The Caucasian Chalk Circle* reflects such a distinction. Not only do Ruddick's ideas point out that mothering is fundamentally cognitive as well as emotional, they highlight material practices in contrast to belief in abstract emotional feelings of love and sacrifice. Ruddick defines the material practices of mothering as preserving, nurturing and training and, as such, also suggests that these are ultimately an anti-war stance since war destroys and annihilates. Brecht's play likewise illuminates this idea; in the midst of war that brings social disintegration, Grusha preserves, nurtures and parents in hopeful action. The narrative of the drama might hinge on the physical test of a mother's love but Grusha's effort might also be considered an anti-war stance through her actions derived from emotional commitment.

Brechtian drama presents the emotions through the narrative and these are explained often in song lyrics as well as demonstrated through a performer's stance in a process of physicalized bodily expression that lends itself to further adaptation into more acrobatic physical theatre. For example, the 1997 production of *The Caucasian Chalk Circle* by Théâtre de Complicité at London's National Theatre was directed as highly physical theatre in the round. Director Simon McBurney's production reflected Brecht's aesthetic style in a set and costumes that visually conveyed hardship and impoverishment. Brecht's play does not require an actor to embody an expression of inner emotional feeling towards a baby in the performance, since even the test of a mother's love is physically demonstrated by how the two female characters are expected to grab hold of the child and pull with force. Yet Juliet Stevenson's Grusha in this production was considered emotionally moving (Taylor 1997). While acting that induces feeling in Brechtian theatre seems to contradict the concepts of *Verfremdungs* and epic theatre, it corresponds with emotional feeling characteristic of late-twentieth-century political theatre. An emotional effect aligns with how subjective experience was being staged in newer political theatre. Twenty-first-century theatre about identity politics in relation to gender, racial and sexual difference conveys feeling as does theatre about the suffering of First Nations people that invites empathy (see Section Two).

What does Brechtian drama and *The Caucasian Chalk Circle* reveal about the politics of theatrical emotions more generally? In some ways, Brecht's ideas about the function of emotions in theatre seem to continue Aristotle's idea that the spectator should think about the narrative except that Brechtian emotions are demonstratively enacted and Brechtian characters are certainly not Aristotle's esteemed tragic characters who do not deserve their fate. Brecht's characters are ignoble and comic despite their serious plight in a destructive world and complicit in unheroic actions and attitudes. They challenge beliefs perpetuated elsewhere in theatre – falsely or otherwise – that morally esteem courage and self-sacrifice. Instead, in Brecht's plays, humanity's emotions appear amoral and outcomes reveal ambiguous motives.

While Brechtian drama reveals how negative emotions impact directly on people's lives in political ways, it remains attuned to a full range of contradictory emotions, and the pleasurable enjoyment of this theatre remains hopeful. Brecht's ideas contradict the belief that emotional feeling is innate and private, and suggest instead that it is social and communal. In this way, theatre theory and drama were predictive of subsequent arguments in the study of the emotions. At the same time, a Brechtian approach highlights the importance of thinking about how emotions reinforce hierarchies of identity in society, and need to be thoughtfully disentangled in depictions of the struggle to achieve equality and justice. Given a late-twentieth-century rejection of a singular platform to bring about political change, as well as the philosophical encouragement of numerous perspectives in multicultural societies, the contradictory emotions of Brechtian drama remain relevant and for later political theatre. Stevens (2016), for example, finds a continuation of Brecht's 'zigzag' dialectic theatre in recent anti-war performance such as *Le Dernier Caravansérail* by the French company, Théâtre du Soleil, and the text *Seven Jewish Children* by Caryl Churchill that seeks to convey the emotional plight of displaced Palestinian people. But Stevens discerns that some of this later performance also responds to conflict with 'anger, frustration, helplessness and cynicism to hope' (2016: 2). While Brecht's ideological certainty has been superseded with scepticism about political events and ambiguous values (Stevens 2016: 204), political performance can still be potent through its illumination of contradictory emotional tensions.

It is possible that Brecht's ideas may have inadvertently led to a lack of attention to, and scholarship about, the emotions in theatre practice. Meg Mumford, for example, suggests that contrary to the widely held view, emotions should be considered part of Brecht's dialectic aesthetic. His use of popular genres, she suggests, means that emotional enjoyment and humorous content become paramount. Mumford writes that 'epic theatre aims to create tensions between an array of emotions' (2009: 64). Perhaps the ways in which emotions are broadly grouped as positive or negative experiences, and pleasurable or otherwise, provide useful categories with which to interpret the emotions in theatrical scenarios and a Brechtian dialectic. As James Thompson recognizes, Brecht understood that emotional feeling and meaning might require different framing for what are termed the practices of '"theatre for pleasure"' and '"theatre for instruction"', but that pleasure and instruction could nonetheless happen simultaneously (2011: 129).

Emotional practice from Forum Theatre to rasaboxes

In contrast to an Aristotelian process of catharsis or a Brechtian approach of educating the audience, Augusto Boal, a performer and director of popular theatre who later became a politician in Brazil, developed a theatre to empower spectators to take action in the theatre and in their social worlds. Boal determines that even Brechtian theatre did not facilitate this possibility and instead develops what he calls 'theatre of the oppressed' through work with marginalized communities in South America and elsewhere. Significantly, Boal criticizes both Stanislavski's and Brecht's realist theatre because of the dominance of fictional characters. For example, Boal describes 'empathy' as 'terrible' because it is passive since the spectator is encouraged to acquiesce to a fictional character (2008: 93). Rather, Boal encourages the audience to intervene and determine what happens next in a short drama about a relevant social problem. He describes this practice as 'Forum Theatre', and today it is used in education and social justice programmes worldwide. As Boal explains of his Forum Theatre, community audiences 'try to enter into dialogue with the actors' and ask for an explanation (2008: 120), which creates an empowering reversal as spectators interrupt to take control and shape the narrative, instruct the actors, and determine appropriate emotional reactions based on their own experiences. In other words, Boal's theatre encourages participants to select and rehearse emotional attitudes in social situations taken from their own lives and to politically redress injustice. Forced to flee from Brazil under military government in 1971, Boal developed Forum Theatre in international contexts such as in Portugal in 1974 with a scene about land ownership with a landowner and evicted agricultural labourers, and different outcomes were dramatized benefitting the labourers (2002: 246). In 2001, in Brazil, Boal worked with the landless workers about their struggle to obtain land by occupying unused land (2002: 7–8). In Turin in Italy, his Forum Theatre was about a young urban couple desperately trying to find a place to live, and the man's low earning capacity was judged against that of a wealthier man who wanted the place part time (2002: 266). The scenario raised questions about what to do and one intervention suggested the couple squat in an unoccupied place. Boal also develops exercises for training performers, and an exercise called 'Analytical Rehearsal of Emotion' involves two actors doing the same scene first with hate, then with love and then qualified with another emotion such as cowardice or impatience (2002: 229).

Western theatre absorbs innovative approaches to the emotions in actor training. In an imaginative synthesis of Brechtian ideas, Stanislavskian approaches, studies of the emotions such as those of Ekman, and performance traditions from India, performance theorist and practitioner Richard Schechner (2001) created an accessible way of working with emotions for performers using what he calls 'rasaboxes'. 'Rasabox' workshop training encourages performers to associate physical action with an emotion and trains participants to move physically in the space to explore an emotion such as anger or fear. Schechner drew on traditional Indian performance training and the idea of *rasa* or emotion that comes from a 2,000-year-old Sanskrit text from India, the *Natyashastra*. This text sets out detailed instructions for performer training and making theatre and it has been highly influential in Indian theatre over millennia. Even though training focused on emotions was atypical in late-twentieth-century Western performance, several teachers created specialized practices. For example, American acting teacher, Susana Bloch, developed a way of physically generating emotion without feeling it (Rix 1998); German actor trainer Stephan Perdekamp's 'PEM' (Perdekamp Emotional Method) technique claims to access a biological process for the performance of emotion. In contrast, Rick Kemp (2012) combines neuroscientific studies with a Stanislavskian-influenced emphasis on the imagination. Schechner's approach also draws extensively on the accumulated theatre theory as well as its practice, and on recent investigations of emotions outside theatre.

Schechner compared the Aristotelian tradition with that of Indian *rasic* performance, and it is clear that *rasa* emotions are not the same as those within lived experience because they are 'knowable, manageable, and transmittable' (2001: 32). What Schechner means here is that emotions are communicated but feelings are subjectively experienced, and *rasa* confirms that performed emotions offer a further distinctive mode – that is, there is a specialized realm of emotional responses in theatre. The concept of *rasa* proposes emotions are shared when a performer induces emotional responses in audience members if not in him/herself. To explain, Ravi Chaturvedi writes that 'the rasa ... are usually considered to be effects, not causes, and are said to come from bhavas' of the mind and body that equate with human emotions, such as love, mirth, sorrow, anger, courage, fear, aversion and wonder (2001: 165, 169–70 note 2). *Rasa* is approached directly with specific physical techniques. Ursula Neuerburg-Denzer describes its Western theatre application as a 'much broader, multi-layered, and at the same time more specific perspective' on the emotions presented and experienced through performance (2014: 78). She reiterates the perspective that performed emotion is communicated between the performer and the spectator, and that these are ideas of emotions as distinct from felt experience that a performer struggles to perform. Neuerberg-Denzer contends that 'in the theatrical context affect should be understood as the most immediate reaction to a stimulus' and not easily managed (2014: 79). Hence both emotional feeling and affect which denote sensation are spontaneous and not easily reproducible, and difficult to realize on demand in performance.

Neuerburg-Denzer draws on the work of neuroscientist Antonio Damasio who investigates the brain-body's physiologies and understands emotional feelings as 'visible and invisible bodily changes in reaction to some kind of trigger event that can range from biochemical processes to skin coloration and facial expression' (Neuerburg-Denzer 2014: 79). While there has been integration of brain science into ideas of cognition in theatre, the focus is on mental processing more than emotional responses (McConachie and Hart 2006). Neuerburg-Denzer points out that neuroscience is showing that there is a momentary delay in self-awareness of bodily experience, and this can inform how performers train their bodily processes to develop an automatic sequence for emotional expression.

A performer learns to voluntarily physicalize what is recognized as the emotions through embodied training practices, and Schechner's 'rasaboxes' approach couples the emotions with movement within the space. In training and/or rehearsal, the performer might reflect on where the sensation of feeling happens in the body – say, in the stomach or through the skin or tingling through the body – and recall it later (Neuerburg-Denzer 2014: 76). Thus, training involves the performer learning to cue bodily indicators of emotional feelings but not necessarily feel them in the moment. This is an expectation common to the practitioners discussed in this section from Aristotle to Diderot, and from Stanislavski to Brecht. Expressive signs are activated mentally and physically by choice, and reinforced by repetition, in preparation for the performance – for example, when a performer is required to cry. Schechner quotes Paula Murray Cole, who was Ofelia for the 1999 production of *Hamlet* which he directed, describing the rasabox training process behind her performance of grief, in which she progresses from deep breathing to changing posture as '"*I sink into the feeling, my eyes well up with tears*"' (2001: 45, italics in original). The open-ended 'rasaboxes' offer a structure within which the performer physically explores what can be communicated in training and rehearsal, and by working with others. This training has the flexibility to accommodate Brecht's position that a performer should physically show the emotions as well as a Stanislavskian-influenced psychophysical preparation for characterization.

A performer practises the emotions for performance by learning about the management of bodily feelings within set patterns and movement that train the emotional processes of the brain-body. This kind of training offers a rich area of exploration in the preparation for nonverbal as well as spoken delivery. An emphasis on physicality offsets the belief that performing emotion depends on retrieving and revealing inner bodily feeling during performance. The progressive development of innovative ways of working with emotion across the twentieth century illustrates how performance adapts to new theory and thinking and creates new forms.

The ways in which theatre offered a heightened emotional experience continued to be evident throughout the twentieth century. As I will explore in the next section, theatre continues to challenge social beliefs about the emotions as it allows the consequences of emotions in life to be recognized and it encourages cognitive evaluation and an appreciation of how subjective feeling is provoked and evokes responses in others. Theatrical performance offers an engagement in which emotions are distilled, and this can seem intense. In short, theatre has a history of configuring emotion to suit its purpose. Herein lies a further paradox indicated by characters who quote from theatre in Chekhov's *The Seagull*: the emotional experience of theatrical performance can be connected to other theatrical experiences as much as to what happens in life.

SECTION TWO

Affect and case studies

Section Two explores the ways in which affect in performance can be distinguished from emotional feeling and in relation to spectator responses and empathy. Theories of affect have proliferated in the twenty-first century, in part because they offer a way of thinking about how the human is intricately connected with the nonhuman world and coupled with technology. Affect theories thereby expand the analysis of live performance to include its use of multimedia and screen technology, and point to an impersonal dimension to feeling.

Case studies illustrate emotional feeling and affect, and these include Henrik Ibsen's classic play, *A Doll's House* (1879), about the break-up of a marriage. The play continues to be produced globally in productions that range from conventional psychological realism and its emotional feeling to nonrealist spectacle evoking affect. Of particular interest is Mabou Mines's nonrealist production *Dollhouse* which evoked affect through its use of popular performance forms ranging from melodrama and pantomime to acrobatic action. The consideration of affect continues with the examples of Stelarc's contemporary live performance and the acrobatic technological spectacle of Cirque du Soleil that both illustrate how performance evokes bodily affect in the absence of psychologies of emotional feeling. The distinction being made here between affect and emotional feeling is intended to broaden understanding of how performance and its multiple visual and aural effects are artistically created and received by spectators. The discussion then considers affects in political performance about real lives in, for example, Anna Deavere Smith's performance.

In recent decades, the evocation of empathy has become a major intention of performance about disadvantage, disability, and racial, ethnic and sexual identity difference. But empathy is widely associated with subjective emotional feeling. In particular, the case study of Jane Harrison's *Stolen* depicting First Nations Aboriginal people and stories of emotional suffering illustrates the ways in which theatre invites the empathetic responses of spectators. The final case study explores the evocation of affect, emotional feeling and empathy in Robert Lepage's productions, *Needles and Opium* (1991/2013) and *887* (2015, Toronto), performances which combine impersonal arresting visual imagery with personal biographical narratives about performative identity and transgressive love.

Emotional feeling to affect in
A Doll's House

Ibsen's *A Doll's House* from 1879 is considered one of his greatest plays and not least because it contributed to the invention of a new realism in theatre. It presents the realistic emotional feelings of a marriage breakdown, and the play's ending was highly controversial in its initial productions because the wife, Nora, leaves. A realistic production of the play involves acting the subjective feeling of the characters in believable ways. Nora is married to bank manager, Torvald Helmer, with three children, and she had borrowed money when Torvald was ill by forging her dying father's signature. She is being blackmailed by the professionally disgraced Nils Krogstad about this secret. He requires her to persuade her husband to give him a position at the bank, but Torvald refuses. Later, as a letter arrives from Krogstad revealing everything, Nora dances the Tarantella under instruction from Torvald and their family friend, Dr Rank, who is dying. After reading the letter, the angry Torvald blames Nora for his pending social ruin because of her actions. Meanwhile Christine Linde, Nora's friend, returning to her hometown as a widow, has renewed a romantic involvement with Krogstad and, learning of Nora's predicament, Christine persuades him to take back his letter. Significantly, Nora had contemplated suicide since she had expected Torvald to assume responsibility for her wrongdoing and fears that he will kill himself. But here Ibsen overturned the convention of nineteenth-century melodrama whereby social shame ended in death. Instead Torvald's angry outburst about his loss of social position unravels Nora's belief in his masculine heroism and her feminine dependency. As they debate ideals of honour and shame in the play, Nora tells Torvald that she is leaving the marriage calmly. In director Carrie Cracknell's 2012 production for London's Young Vic Theatre, however, Nora's realization of Torvald's weakness turned into explosive anger. The twenty-first-century production updates Nora's emotional response to include anger.

A Doll's House depicts emotionally intimate exchanges that happen in private in the public space of theatre. In acknowledging theatre as a '"public feeling project"', Erin Hurley points to how concepts of felt experience separate into intimate and private, versus public and shared, but are made to intersect within realist Western theatre (2014: 3). A character situated in a domestic setting is assumed to be revealing personal feeling within his or her private world; simultaneously this is happening in theatre, which is a depersonalized public space. Hence feeling spaces converge; in its complicated conceptualization, theatre sets up a belief that these spaces of feeling exist concurrently.

The lasting significance of Ibsen's play comes from its depiction of a female character who leaves an unequal relationship in order to discover a sense of self, thereby placing this need before that of her family. In 1879, it was shocking that a mother would choose to leave her marriage and children, and a woman leaving her children continues to be socially relevant to contemporary audiences. A fear of social rejection is a common theme in Ibsen's drama, reflecting, as Michael Goldman (1999) explains, the values of nineteenth-century European society, and as Torvald angrily blames Nora, it is Nora who overcomes the fear of social judgement. Nora overrides attachment to her family as well as fear of the unknown. Recent productions of the play have centred on Nora as emblematic of women's emancipation in more modern times (Holledge et al. 2016: 9). As Julie Holledge, Jonathan Bollen, Frode Helland and Joanne Tompkins point out, the play about Nora's courage has become a global success, a Norwegian export experienced through thousands of productions including Cracknell's, and they suggest that as the play's reputation grew, its legacy of diverse productions came to reflect '"persistence, variation, and memory"', a multicultural memory of theatre's capacity to challenge convention (2016: 20).

The character of Nora must literally perform within the play: initially she does so with an emotionally pleasing persona, and later through what Torvald describes as dancing in madness (Ibsen 1982: 77). Nora's fast swirling movement conveys her emotional turmoil. In addition, Torvald describes his own performative fantasies of her as his 'secret mistress', 'huntress' and 'temptress' (Ibsen 1982: 88). This role-playing and imaginative fantasy equates sexual and emotional relationships with theatre; as Nora performs emotionally to please Torvald, he is both a director and a spectator. This points to a performer carrying out emotion work (or labour) to please an audience (Solga 2019). In the play Nora changes from delivering a highly emotive performance aligned with her feminine identity to presenting a calm thoughtful demeanour in her honest exchange with Torvald at the end. In its progression from Nora's emotional frivolity to reasoned decision-making, the play challenges the belief that women are more emotional than rational.

A Doll's House concludes with the door closing (often in production, slamming) behind Nora. This dramatic moment has led to both realist and nonrealist theatrical responses that imagine what happens to Nora after she leaves. Lucas Hnath's *A Doll's House, Part 2* (2017, South Coast Repertory, Costa Mesa, and then the John Golden Theatre on Broadway) depicted the emotional feelings of an exuberant, fulfilled Nora fifteen years later. She had become a successful writer because of her experience, but has to return to a dignified Torvald and nanny, Anne Marie, still living in the household because Torvald had not divorced Nora, rendering her professional writing contracts illegal. I viewed the Melbourne Theatre Company production of *Part 2* (14 August 2018) which depicted Torvald (Greg Stone) as solemn but sad, and Nora (Marta Dusseldorp) as excited but anxious about her visit, describing how she overcame isolation and despair after she left. It showed Nora as hopeful, but Hnath's intricate plot depicted Nora's daughter, Emmy, in love and about to marry a banker following the pattern of Nora's early life and willing to forge Nora's death certificate to protect her father who had benefitted from letting everyone believe Nora was dead. If this version suggested that Nora's emotional struggle also awaited her daughter, it allowed Nora to foresee a future of freer emotional relationships for both women and men as she left once again. Hnath's updated play reaffirmed Nora's capacity to reflect women's struggle for equality in their intimate emotional relationships as well as in their social roles.

Drama and theatre continued to delve into the psychology of characters throughout the twentieth century (Cody and Sprinchorn 2007), explaining the emotional feelings through the dialogue and interactions. In keeping with ideas of an emotional self (Lupton 1998), realistic theatre presents a character's expression of subjective emotional feeling to other characters and thus to audiences (Tait 2002). For example, the characters in Anton Chekhov's *The Seagull* describe how they feel, and by using analogous examples from literature and drama, characters present the descriptions of other fictional characters in order to explain their feelings. By implication, emotional feelings are socially explained by reference to those performed in theatrical performance and cinema. This aligns with a philosophical proposition that the emotional subjectivity of another cannot be directly experienced and becomes known through a process of confession. As well, Chekhov's characters verbally describe a phenomenology of the body's feeling that set precedents for later drama, such as that of Samuel Beckett (Tait 2002; Luckhurst and Tait 2019; Lehmann 2007). In a twenty-first-century ultra-lifelike interpretation, English director Katie Mitchell, who focuses on emotional expression in performance (Shirley 2018), created a controversial production of *The Seagull* in 2007 at London's National Theatre with key actors portraying characters who mumbled so they seemed completely self-absorbed which shifted the emphasis away from drawing out audience feeling. Theatrical performance explains and models subjective experience for spectators and in this way makes emotional feelings meaningful for contemporary audiences within the public space of theatre.

The process of making classic plays relevant to twenty-first-century audiences is also evident in the type of spectator responses that are invited and the shift from an evocation of emotional feeling to affect. An imaginative interpretation of Ibsen's *A Doll's House* in Mabou Mines' *Dollhouse* encompassed nonrealistic forms and elaborated on the central idea by placing a doll-wife constrained in a doll's house set with miniaturized furniture. Exaggerated visual and aural elements elicited felt sensation and the production suggested how a spectator might bodily respond without necessarily becoming emotionally engaged. The company describes turning Ibsen's feminism into 'a parable of scale' through visible contrasts (Mabou Mines). Adapted by Maude Mitchell and Lee Breuer, and directed by Breuer in 2003, Mabou Mines' *Dollhouse* toured internationally for a decade. Susan Bennett describes how most filmed versions heighten the play's naturalism (1990: 153–60), in contrast to the filmed version of Mabou Mines' production that captured a nonrealist interpretation (*Mabou Mines' Dollhouse* 2008). In this visually striking production, the female characters appeared too big in the doll's house set, which was proportional for the performers of short stature cast as the male characters. Actor Mark Povinelli, who played Torvald, is 3 feet 9 inches (114.3 centimetres) and 'refers to himself as a "little person"' and acknowledges that he has the biological 'condition of dwarfism' which limits his height, and Povinelli explains "'physicality affects every aspect of my life' including professional roles"' (quoted in Fisher 2007). He recognizes that little people working as professional theatre and film actors look back at a history of sideshow performance; activism in recent decades promotes inclusive employment practices. The controversial casting for social inclusiveness by the Mabou Mines company facilitated a particular aesthetic effect that graphically illuminated the disparity in gender roles. Breuer took the cue for casting from a production directed by Bertolt Brecht, in which short actors played the army leaders and thus caricatured the military, although Breuer's production set out to caricature the patriarchy instead (*Looking for a Miracle* 2008).

The contrasts in size and scale impacted on sensory responses and therefore on spectator affect. In Mitchell and Breuer's production, Nora (Maude Mitchell) behaved as a childish tease, emotional manipulator, and seductress, in exaggerated ways, to demonstrate the contradictions surrounding a woman performing to maintain her position as wife and mother. This reflects Brecht's approach encouraging emotions that are demonstrated and physicalized in gesture and posture. At times Mitchell's vocal delivery was in a child-like high pitch and in scenes with Kristine Linde (Janet Girardeau), and Nora appeared in bird-like movement to demonstrate a caged existence and at other times carrying a doll as a child substitute. As she danced around the set, Nora tried to please in ways that became increasingly ridiculous and particularly when Torvald shouted angrily at her. She picked him up lovingly in her arms; the image was used to promote the filmed version (*Mabou Mines' Dollhouse* 2008). In this radical revision of the play, exaggerated gender role difference was visible and held up to ridicule.

The performers appeared cartoon-like as they reproduced the play's dialogue and interactions with Brechtian interruptions. They critiqued cultural identity when, at one point, the female musician of Asian American heritage (Ning Yu or Susan Tang), who had been playing the piano throughout, got up and walked out, offended, after Torvald described women holding knitting needles as being clumsy and like a 'damned Chinaman' (Ibsen 1982: 86). The performers came out of role and called out to the musician, 'it's in the text', and she came back. In this action, the distressing racism of the character's lines was counteracted by the direct intervention of the performers. In a documentary about the making of the film version, *Looking for a Miracle*, directed by Reiner Moritz (2008), Breuer explained that he adopted a Brechtian historical approach rather than bring the play into a contemporary context since Nora's coquettish behaviour about money seemed dated in an era when women everywhere are now in paid employment. Breuer advocated detachment in viewing and pointed out that removing the realism created comic twists, and allowed for parody and in the emotional expression. The documentary contained interviews with the actors: Povinelli insightfully explaining Torvald; Mitchell perceptively describing Nora; and Margaret Lancaster explaining the maid Helene's pregnancy.

The film of the production replicated the spatial arrangement of conventional theatre but presented a doll-like audience as a single entity, facial expressions changing in unison. This encouraged viewers to consciously question the accepted idea of regimented spectatorship and reflect instead on its potential for disunity. Replicating nineteenth-century costuming, the production used diverse theatrical forms including pantomime, opera, slapstick action, mask, puppets and magic to reinforce the play's idea of tricks, as well as singing and stylized dancing.

Hence the choice of theatrical forms meant exaggerating the expression of emotional feeling. Krogstad (Kristopher Medina) appeared costumed as a melodramatic villain in an oversized top-hat, and there were also hints of the sideshow and even circus as characters acrobatically rolled in and out of boxes – acrobatics underlie all circus. A dream turned into a nightmare as Dr Rank (Ricardo Gil) appeared in a mask of death pursuing Nora around the stage in farcical action, a reaction to her flirtatious engagement. The oversized pregnant maid made the inequity of her domestic labour and reproductive labour apparent in the middle-class household and where a maid's powerless social position rendered her susceptible to predatory male behaviour. The ensuing social shame and disgrace for a working woman like the maid could not remain private and was outwardly visible. In a Brechtian approach, the material circumstances of the maid's plight were apparent and the accompanying emotional feelings were inferred rather than enacted. Throughout, the exaggerated display indicative of older theatrical genres framed but distanced the emotional expression as it highlighted the social circumstances that created them.

The actor showed the character and the production visually highlighted the symbolic value of the power relationships. The performers frequently came out of role to perform additional movement and action in a range of theatrical genres and performed emotions. When Torvald proclaimed how corruption arises from wives who lie and poison their world, and become depraved, the character's speech conveyed anger as a masculine prerogative in an emotional tirade against women having emotional power over men. Nora has been playing the role to emotionally please Torvald, but spectators knew that Nora had only lied to help him out of love, so that the dramatic irony of Torvald's self-righteous claims that such people make him physically sick, turned him into a figure of delusion. As well, a spectator observed the way that Nora became increasingly out of control in her movement and gesture as the narrative progressed to a carnivalesque climax. Nora's behaviour implied that the controlled pleasing demeanour of feminine identity was unravelling under the threat of Krogstad's revelations, and the dancing physically manifested her emotional distress as hysteria.

Christina Wald's (2007) analysis of the physical symptoms of hysteria and a contrasting melancholia in drama points out that while these no longer constitute types of psychiatric diagnosis of individual suffering as they did in nineteenth-century medicine, the concepts remain a source of fascination in the arts. Wald considers emotionally graphic depictions of such conditions in English language drama and its theatre as a 'cultural trope' of trauma (2007: 3) – trauma does coincide with the current medical diagnosis of post-traumatic stress disorder. A prevalence of female hysterical characterization becomes apparent in drama outlining resistance to the social control of emotions whereby selective emotional expression underlies the appearance of gender normality. In addition, hysteria in theatrical performance reveals the alignment of cultural ideas of extreme emotionality, femininity and madness. The paradox of hysterical symptoms that are physically embodied, however, is that the dramatic content reveals how characters 'are installed in psychic repetition compulsions' through their involuntary condition that cannot be bodily controlled; in contrast, the theatrical performance involves repetition that is deliberately and intentionally enacted including loss of control (Wald 2007: 20). Wald points out that this divergence contradicts Judith Butler's idea of gender performativity as concealment. Theatrical performance imitates hysteria in its overt embodied display, but what is more challenging to enact is the opposite which is a diffused type of internalized distress that denotes feminine identity and emotional self-control to maintain gendered norms. Within Freudian psychoanalytic approaches, femininity is associated with lack in relation to phallic masculinity, which turns into a type of mourning for the self's incompleteness, and fuels suppression accompanied by unhappiness.

The 'doing' of gender in the stabilizing of difference that Judith Butler (2004a) theorizes as performative identity implicates melancholia in the delineation of femininity. Melancholic feeling is an internalized response to symbolic and actual powerlessness in society and it may be unconscious. Sigmund Freud makes a distinction between mourning due to grief over the loss of someone or something and melancholia which is not as specific yet 'somatic' and bodily sustained (1914–16: 243–4). But if Butler initially excluded theatre from performative identity and feminine melancholia because theatre involves intentional choices about identity rather than unconscious responses, at the same time theatre does not necessarily consciously challenge gender identity's division of the emotions. The performance of emotions in theatre can reinforce gender difference. Traditionally, for example, while feminine identity aligned with overt emotionality and masculinity with a more stoic demeanour, male characters could display anger but females expressed sadness, vulnerability and distress. In practice, theatrical performance ranges from the unreflective deployment of stereotypical femininity and its tearfulness and hysteria and/or masculinity with its coolness and anger to careful deliberation on the unconventional emotional depiction of gender. In Mabou Mines' *Dollhouse*, exaggeration exposed mechanisms of performative identity through the embodied contrasts as it revealed the gendered premise behind emotional excess and hysteria.

Most of *Dollhouse* had a direct sensory effect through its nonrealistic staging without inviting an emotionally felt response, that is, until towards the end. The distorted proportions induced awareness of visual engagement, even optic discomfort – that is, bodily sensation. While the staging evoked affect in Acts one and two, the possibility of an emotionally felt response emerges in Act three as Nora's well-intended deception is revealed. Spectators might have responded with both bodily affect and personal emotional feeling to how Torvald physically hit Nora or reacted to how tears flowed from them both as the revelations, and accusations unfolded. As Nora realized that they were not who she believed them to be, the Mabou Mines characters removed their costumes as if the characters were taking off their gender and social artifice. In a prolonged ending which was interspersed with operatic song, the performers literally stripped, left the stage slowly, Nora walking away naked with a shaven head. The tone of the production completely changed, and the intensity of the ending invited compassion for both characters. The final segment confirms that an emotionally felt response might only happen in one part of a production; in this instance, as it turned into a harrowing evocation of the anguish and rawness at the end of a relationship.

It is being argued here that affect and emotional feeling can be artistically distinguished and to appreciate complex patterns of embodied engagement. As indicated theatrical performance and acrobatic circus induce bodily feeling and become a powerful force independent of cognitive understanding. Other types of feeling in theatre can be due to its immediacy, encapsulated by concepts of intensity and performer presence (Goodall 2008). Unquestionably, theatrical performance evokes a range of felt responses successfully and repeatedly; it also takes advantage of how feeling can be contagious in a group. This achievement, however, implicates all the artistic elements of production that surround performers, including sound and lighting. It might be technical elements of the production and/or the music that partly stir feelings, and through their combined impact (see Section Three).

Theatre's sensory environment elicits felt sensations. Martin Welton (2012) points out that theatre scholarship has appreciated the dimension of sensory experience in performance since the 1970s when practitioners such as Jerzy Grotowski claimed that a shared experience arises with intense visual and aural performance to create a type of (temporary) community (see Section Three). The claim that an intense sensory experience unifies an audience sits uneasily with reception theory that acknowledges difference in spectator backgrounds. As Welton explains, however, there is a common embodied experience as most theatre happens spatially within an auditorium that creates a separate sensory world with darkness and silence, and therefore meaning is created within such environments. In his analysis of feeling in practice-based performance, Welton outlines a biological impetus behind theatre's sensory perception and, which he points out, arises within the movement created by performance (2012: 2). Welton argues that perceiving 'movement of "information" *about* movement might well be glossed simply as its "feeling"' but how a spectator '*gets* a feel' for a performance illuminates that 'feel' can be both a verb and a noun (2012: 3, 4, italics in original). He does make a distinction between different types of feeling but within an active unfolding process of convergence.

Affect refers to physical responsiveness through felt sensation and including the bodily pulses accompanying thought and it implies that sensing and feeling are inseparable and unavoidable. But even bodily experience of performance can be highly variable. The biological functions of the sensory body and sensing brain are involved in such processes (Di Benedetto 2010). Yet this has an inadvertent side effect of suggesting biological determinism in bodily responses and that all bodies function in the same way and towards emotional stimuli in performance. Rather this theoretical idea of biological sameness can be offset by acknowledgement of embodied diversity. For example, the sensory orientation of spectators to movement becomes complicated by the way they bring diverse physical training experience, from dance to sports, to how they watch performers in movement. Interpretations expand into numerous possible individual combinations and variations of feeling. While it can be presumed that spectator feeling connects life and theatre, lives differ greatly. Accordingly, it can be argued that while sensory responses to performance implicate the body's biology, even brain-body physiological capacities develop over time in divergent ways.

Affect and technology: Live art and spectacle

Contemporary performance, in association with an expanded field of live art with a strong visual impact, developed from the late twentieth century and corresponds more with ideas of affect than an emotional effect. Brian Massumi (2002) points out that

Stelarc, who places his body at the centre of his performance art, expands human biology with a range of technological parts and seems like a cyborg with the addition of a prosthesis and the operation of involuntary movement of his body wired up to the internet and moved by computers located across the world (Dixon 2007). Massumi writes that 'the activation of information operates through the sensitization of the human body-matter to electromagnetic *force*', and Stelarc pushes this capacity to extreme limits in the 'transformed return of sensation' (2002: 123–4, 125, italics in original). In this way, the affect of the performing body is changed and Stelarc's performance demands an embodied response from a viewer watching him live or on a screen. Responses may be more about sensations of discomfort and squeamishness; there is no expectation of emotional sympathy for a character/persona. Scientific knowledge and technological practices, including the embodied practices of artists such as Stelarc, require a wider explanation of human responsiveness, which the concept of affect allows. Massumi also gives examples of the affect of television programmes and sport and how the home viewing space sets up a new type of 'belonging' (2002: 83). Leaving emotional loyalty to a particular sports team aside, Massumi is proposing that the affects arising from watching sport circulate in and blend into other broadcast media and imagery transmission. The consumption of electronic media flows together in viewer reception.

Ideas of sensation in viewer responses to visual art and live performance might seem to revive historical associations with sensibility from the eighteenth and nineteenth centuries except that the twenty-first-century explanation of affect is emphasizing bodily processes as instrumental in how meaning is transmitted and received. It reflects twenty-first-century concepts of interconnection and convergence in contrast to earlier ideas of selective sensibilities and separation within a social hierarchy. Moreover, ideas of affect elaborate on the ways in which technological processes contribute to lived experience, for example, in the increased reliance of the human world on hand-held mobile phones and invisible wireless. Nonetheless, in consideration of performance, a technological spectacle can elicit strong tingling and visceral reactions such as breath holding and stomach tightening that is outside a person-to-person transmission since the technology offers an impersonal force field. An example of a live technological production that induces affect and avoids emotional psychologies, and which has toured internationally, is provided by Cirque du Soleil's (Cirque) live show, *Toruk, The First Flight*, an adaptation of imagery from the animated 2009 film, *Avatar*, directed by James Cameron. Cirque's integration of live circus acrobatic and aerial action, puppetry and lighting with large-scale, digitized filmed projection created an entertainment spectacle for the twenty-first century and was viewed on 2 November 2017 at the Rod Laver Arena, Melbourne. Acrobatic action heightens the bodily impact of a performance – as it did for one part of Mabou Mines *Dollhouse*. *Toruk* was intended as a nonhuman fantasy world, and while the original cinematic source about conflict and war depicted animated faces with emotional responses, these were not part of the live arena spectacle with its diminutive performers. Instead in the live *Toruk* show, humanoid figures in blue leotard costumes with tails and painted blue skin appeared miniaturized amidst enormous nonhuman tree footings created by electronic projections to fill a large sports stadium. The opening idyll of the distant acrobats tumbling and climbing vine ropes in an evergreen jungle, and in sports games, or drumming suspended from up high, suggested a world where the only threat was the legendary flying dragon-like toruk, a mechanized puppet in the show. It gave way to initiation rites with a shaman instructing three teenage heroes to obtain sacred talismans from each of the five tribes in order to save the tree of souls. This simplistic narrative might have been widely dismissed, but it was completely subordinate to the purpose of offering a visual spectacle, which remained impressive throughout. For example, the sacred tree appeared as delicate hanging willow-like strands of white light. As the two males and one female sought to obtain the talismans, they journeyed through tribal worlds where dancers evoked fragrances while giant fans of orange-red fabric folded in and out around their bodies as wings; acrobats contorted and balanced like insects on a large skeleton; formations of warriors clambered up and down tall swaying poles; and swooping creatures flew far above electronic ocean waves. Strange mechanical animal puppets appeared and included fantastic hounds, horses, tortoises and reptilian birds, and one of the three teenagers finally rode on the back of the toruk to save their world. *Toruk* had a continuous soundscape of music and a voiced narrative – an element that most earlier Cirque shows did not include. While bodies in circus have a strong sensory impact with risky acrobatic action inducing visceral thrill, an emotional feeling such as excitement is a side effect rather than enacted, one enhanced by technical effects. But Cirque's *Toruk* production elevated the technical effects, and it was the large-scale projected visual imagery that was the most inventive element with waterfalls appearing along with rivers and oceans washing across the arena floor. This live show with its simulation of flying and falling was intended to induce strong sensory affect and the production filled the space with depersonalized effects. Its cognitive meaning was unimportant. Visceral sensation might have varied in intensity, but it was difficult to avoid. A scene depicting an earthquake involved distant performers in abseiling harnesses climbing up and falling from a rock face of falling rocks and this proved particularly potent in its sensory engagement. Undeniably, the impersonally generated technological spectacle had a bodily impact on spectators – as cinema can. Some sudden affective jolts, such as in response to falling climbers, may have been involuntary.

The crucial point about affect is that it can be impersonal. It is broader than an emotional feeling, which is invariably associated with a personal response. Massumi and Brennan recognize that bodily affect can be impersonal, by which they mean that it might arise in an environment and not be instigated by, or attached to, the presence of someone else. This idea of impersonal affect complicates analysis of affect in theatrical performance. Performance theory encompassing recent interdisciplinary concepts of affect engages with a sensitivity to movement and currents at a cellular level – concepts clearly aligned with scientific knowledge. But theatrical performance typically involves human-to-human exchange, whereas affect can also refer to a solitary encounter with the nonhuman and even an absence of humans.

The extent to which a spectator engages with the facial and bodily expression of the performer is arguable. In relation to impersonal affect, it is possible to theorize that the performer(s) might not be the source of affective responses and that such responses potentially arise from the elements of production and the overall effect, for example, with the projected imagery in *Toruk*. Music and lighting technologies in theatre production contribute to the evocation of affect as well as emotional feeling. An explanation of audience affect in relation to an actual theatrical performance needs to be cautiously interpreted, given diverse embodied responses to movement and the way the audience itself enhances the affect of the physical space.

Real identities and political affect

Ideas of affect in performance present complex possibilities to illuminate and complicate cognitive meaning and especially the way performance with a political purpose is received. As Elin Diamond, Denise Varney and Candice Amich explain, 'Affect guides us to think of new forms of relationality conducive to exploring the many vectors of feeling aroused by performance' (2017: 4). They value its interactive energetic capacity and point out that it is the affect arising through radical performance addressing major political concerns which can be particularly powerful. This is performance that illuminates political meaning through its affective impressions. In linking affect theory to performance, Elin Diamond explains that it shifts 'the focus from the individual and personal, from discourse and constructivism to skin-level intensities that pass impersonally between and among bodies, human or non-human' (2017: 259). While celebrating the possibilities of unstructured affect and ideas of performance as assemblages of bodies and objects in space, Diamond questions whether there might not be a loss of cognitive clarity and political impact.

The discussion of affect in theatrical performance here recognizes that affective feeling includes the embodied process of thinking. Performance also commonly involves personification of some kind and implicates personal perception and thought and these personal dimensions need to be considered along with the theoretical tenets of impersonal affect.

Late-twentieth-century theatrical performance that expanded the possibility of politicized affect through the embodiment of diverse racial, ethnic and sexual identities often framed these with auto/biographical narratives that invited identification with them. A relevant question for political performance becomes: to what extent does the affect evoked by theatrical performance connect to the affect of lived experience? It is suggested here that the presentation of real identities and their personal experience in performance creates continuity with the affects of lived experience inclusive of impersonal affect.

The potential of performance to bridge socially diverse actual identities is demonstrated in the brilliantly versatile, solo performances of Anna Deavere Smith, who performed across race, gender and age. Smith who is of African-American heritage, created documentary verbatim theatre that enacted 'multiple crossings' of gender and race through an astoundingly clever mimicry of the movement, gesture, speech and vocal tone of those she interviewed, and then performed (Kondo 2000: 96). In *Fires in the Mirror*, available on film, Smith performed the African-American, Jewish men and middle-aged white policemen involved in the 1991 riots in Brooklyn, New York, presenting their words and perspectives (Smith 1999; Paterson 2015). After a car accident in which a Jewish driver killed an African-American boy, the local community protested and an Australian-Jewish student was fatally attacked. Smith expressly highlights differences by becoming these individuals, and, staged in succession, the emotionally fuelled words of someone involved in the event were juxtaposed with an opposing perspective. Smith invited understanding of diverse perspectives as she enacted community members including white authority figures – she embodied American presidents in *House Arrest*. The process of listening to conflicting viewpoints instigated by *Fires in the Mirror* remains relevant in a world of polarized and entrenched opposition and argument.

In an approach that follows after Brecht's ideas of separation in theatre, the performance detached the representation of subjective experience from its corresponding embodiment, which additionally disturbed an idea that the body-self is a unified entity. Jill Dolan specifies Smith's work as full of hopeful moments that reveal what the world could be as she 'recaptures, reperforms, on her own body, the speech and gestures and something of the essence of the people' who are completely opposite to her own visible identity in theatre and to present diverse perspectives of a social conflict for better understanding (2008: 39, 84). Smith was visually different to the real-life personae who she embodied so that the political significance of this divergence provoked thought and its affect. Smith's performance is being located within Dolan's 'utopian performatives' which are 'small but profound moments' that in the 'doing' provide spectators with a 'hopeful feeling' for a changed life through 'emotionally voluminous, generous, aesthetically striking, and intersubjectively intense' experiences during performance (2008: 5).

The question of where to locate felt experience in a performance is complicated as Smith reveals. Her physical performance of multiple identities invites spectator affect and, at the same time, the short biographical cameos recount emotionally inflicted experience. Smith explains, her performance text is developed through external physicality and repetition rather than concern with interiority such as that evident in Method acting (Kondo 2000: 96). Smith confirmed that the performer was not feeling the emotional feeling described in the verbatim script. As explained in Section One, a performer is not expected to feel the feelings that are conveyed by the text while enacting them. But performer affect happens in the present moment of the performance – bodily sensation being ever present while emotional feeling arises more intermittently.

The powerful impact of Smith's performance also lay in the affects arising from watching her vocally and physically enact someone with a different race and/or gender. Admiration for Smith's extraordinary mimetic capacity and achievement, however, could become mixed up with the uncertainty about how to sensorily absorb this doubling of identity. The oscillating visual transformations in Smith's performance confronted belief in the self's embodied separation from the other. An affective disturbance may arise irrespective of thought; theatrical performance can meet unexpected embodied resistances. The affects arising from Smith's *Fires in the Mirror* were imbued with political significance as the performance undermined perceptions that bodily identity of the other was fixed and separate.

A completely different type of politicized affect was elicited by Mike Bartlett's (2016) absurdist political play, *Wild*, based on well-known figures opposed to the increasing technological control of the nation state. *Wild* was amusing which prefigured an idea of amusement that ranges from the affects of diversion to feelings of mirth. While ostensibly warning about Western democracies and the secret risks of technology, the play centred on the fictional character of Andrew, who is in exile in a Russian hotel room in circumstances that closely parallel those of Edward Snowden, a whistle-blower who exposed the electronic surveillance of the citizens of the United States by its government. The dialogue referred to Julian Assange and a technological precedent set by Assange and WikiLeaks in publicly posting classified official government documents on the internet. These biographical threads in *Wild* highlighted the widespread secret government surveillance of citizens under the justification of maintaining national security. The release of classified documents meant Snowden and Assange contravened United States law. In *Wild*, the affect of digital technology converges with the affect created by a performance as real events became comical despite Andrew's apparent fear for his safety, when he does not know what is happening and who he is dealing with – this also points to public confusion. *Wild* invited amused interest rather than emotional sympathy as it confronted serious political issues. But as a strategy of public engagement, the absurdist interpretation was able to draw attention to nation-state surveillance and the ensuing controversies about loss of privacy. Humorous twists and turns in the narrative highlighted how digital spying allows the exchanges and potentially even the thoughts of citizens to be closely monitored.

Although completely different in their aesthetic effect and cognitive significance, *Fires in the Mirror* and *Wild* elicited affect in relation to real political concerns. While containing descriptions of emotional feeling, each performance sidestepped its realistic enactment and invited engagement within an 'affective register' arising from political circumstances in the wider world (Thompson 2011). These examples suggest ways in which live performance might be relevant to the consideration of affective flows more broadly.

Wild points to how the monitoring of dissident groups can involve the blocking of personal communication in the virtual sphere. Even though the technological circumstances that led to this type of political control might be impersonal, such political processes manifest in the experience of individuals, and often in political persecution and embodied punishment. Performance and visual art draw attention to the political conditions that lead to individual experiences of imprisonment and trauma (Duggan 2012; Trezise 2014). This type of political performance engages directly with embodied feeling. Its impact has become aligned with ideas of evoking empathy.

Empathy enabled: Empathy Museum to Back to Back

An emphasis on empathy in performance has developed alongside the discernment of affect in the twenty-first century. As indicated in the Introduction, definitions of empathy involve thought and most, but not all, include emotional feeling (Coplan and Goldie 2011: xxiii). The participatory performance created by the UK-based Empathy Museum, *A Mile in My Shoes*, involved spectators wearing the shoes of someone else while listening to an autobiographical audio recording. Spectators entered a pop-up box installation set up to resemble a shop with shelves of shoe boxes and were allocated a pair of shoes to walk around in, sometimes awkwardly. The sensations of wearing the shoes of another are experienced through bodily affect. As a wonderful realization of the colloquial phrase about being empathetic and 'walking in the shoes of another', the project created by Clare Patey sought to offset prejudice and conflict by developing empathy through an experiential encounter. It invited individual responses to stories which could be emotionally charged and these stories remain available on the internet as podcasts (Empathy Museum n.d.).

A focus on empathy sits uneasily under affect because of assumptions that empathy involves emotionally felt responses. Impersonal affect remains feasible within a type of involuntary bodily response, but empathy in response to biographical accounts of trauma is presumed to be voluntary and subjective. Stories in performance encouraging an empathetic response are frequently emotionally charged.

An artistic process need not contain a story or narrative and still encourage empathetic responses, and Susan Leigh Foster (2010) thoughtfully discerns how dancers choreograph in ways that arouse empathy through abstract kinetic movement. Jill Bennett (2005) finds that the felt sensations evoked by visual arts can achieve what she terms 'empathetic vision' in the overlap of seeing and feeling in her analysis of art's 'affective truth' of trauma, which does not present a narrative. Bennett explains that responses can be felt as much as recognized with cognition and that visual art and performance in particular engage via the arousal of feeling ranging from the affect of shock to empathy. Bryoni Trezise considers how performance creates cultural memory by manifesting trauma through bodily presence and 'feel-ability' that seeks 'to arrest, repeat and rehearse traumatic affect' (2014: 3). Trauma in theatrical performance is presented either through the personal stories of individuals or through embodied presence and action to evoke empathetic responses.

The complexity surrounding the evocation of empathy raises questions about its effectiveness in social engagement and whether the ideals of greater understanding are realized. This questioning is apparent in one recent performance about disability (the differently abled) that confronts the expectations of spectators. Bree Hadley cites Bill Shannon describing the crushing '"Weight of Empathy"' that descends on him when he does not respond to the well-meaning gestures of others as expected in public space for reasons to do with his difference (2014: 89). Shannon, an athletic physical theatre performer, is frequently asked if he needs help in some contexts but refuses. An initial empathetic response turns into a dissatisfaction with rejection in the social exchange. As Hadley points out, the person with a visible disability is constantly on show in social interactions, as if performing (2014: 1). A viewer projects onto Shannon curiosity about what it feels like to be him. At the same time, Thomas Fahy (2012) contends that disability should be visible in society rather than out of sight. Performance draws attention to performer bodies and Shannon's performance also confronted how spectators predicted physical actions and what people '"phenomenologically intend"' (Hadley 2014: 91). When he moved to pick up an object, someone pre-empted his movement and assisted him, which turned this everyday task into spectacle. It suggested the physiological and mirror neuron response discussed in studies of empathy as well as an accompanying emotional attitude based on imagined subjective substitution. While Shannon's approach might be criticized because the performance was invisible to bystanders, it exposed the socially polite but formulaic reaction that was accorded disability and often interpreted as empathy. Such set responses disempower and Shannon rejected the way his individual agency was being overlooked in the social engagement.

Although most people will experience some form of temporary disablement during their lives, Hadley reiterates that ongoing disability allows the non-disabled body to conceptualize 'what it is not' (2014: 6). A process of naming, categorization, objectification and also imagining calls forth what Emmanuel Levinas describes as violent negation of the other, and her or his (their) subjectivity (Hadley 2014: 7). This happens because the 'ablist society' stares at the disabled body. As Rosemarie Garland Thomson explains, '"The disabled body is not only the medium but the content of the performance"' (quoted in Fahy 2012: x).

But the type of social gathering created by live performance can offset a process of curious objectification and distancing of the other body and/or condition as well as contribute innovatively to the art form. This became apparent in the theatres of the 'deaf' that developed from the 1970s, depictions of blindness in drama, and recent circus and theatre by artists with a physical disability. Contemporary theatre can shift the appraisal of disability from that of fascinated discomfort and sometimes pity to that of artistic appreciation and empathetic connection. It can also challenge a spectator's unthinking expectation of a grateful response.

In her interviews with actors with a physical disability, Lilah Morris (2012) explains that they prefer to be cast in conventional roles such as in Shakespearean productions because, like all actors, they do not want to be typecast. For example, in the 2016 Belvoir Street production of *Twelfth Night*, Keith Robinson, an accomplished actor who uses a wheelchair due to illness, was cast for his acting ability and gave Feste a lively dynamic and innovative characterization that enhanced the whole production (see Section One). His performance changed the aesthetic impact as it gave greater poignancy to Feste's lines as the character observing rather than participating in the romantic liaisons.

In her analysis of how disability has been staged in realist theatre, Kirsty Johnston finds practices that perpetuate social categorization of an 'individual condition' which obscures the 'social and cultural context' for inclusion and exclusion (2016: 18). Drawing on some of the major scholars in this field – Rosemarie Garland Thomson, Petra Kuppers, Carrie Sandahl, Bruce Henderson and Anna Hickey Moody – Hadley explains how contemporary performance inverts the historical sideshow practices in which spectatorship turned disability and difference into freak shows (Hadley 2014: 11–12). Art and performance that reflects the disability rights movement often seeks to avoid the autobiographical trajectory of what happened and how that individualizes and personalizes rather than politicizes (Hadley 2014: 9–10). The realness of the performance is intended to provoke the self-reflection of spectators by expanding on elements of uncertainty and shifting spectators from a conventional response to seeing the disability to perceiving the person. The performance seeks to have an impact on the personal perspectives of spectators.

Artists therefore utilize the possibilities of surprise to catch audiences off guard. Back to Back Theatre's performance includes tactical interventions in public spaces indicative of immersive theatre (Machon 2013). The Back to Back ensemble consists of performers with intellectual disabilities and includes long-time collaborators Simon Laherty, Sarah Mainwaring and Scott Price working with director, Bruce Gladwin, and it is very well known in Australia and internationally (Grehan and Eckersall 2013). The production *Small Metal Objects* from 2005 explored the theme of monetary value from coins to abstract economic concepts, and the exclusion of differently abled people from work and economic systems, and it was performed in crowded public spaces such as train stations. Spectators had to try to find the performers among the crowd while they listened to their conversations through headphones. They heard snippets about a party and drugs in humorous miscommunication, and the performers were not immediately visible in the public spaces in the same way that their disabilities may not be evident. *Small Metal Objects* required the spectators to be active participants in the event and with its implicit empathetic message about the right of those with a disability to be in public space, and without undue attention (Hadley 2014: 82–7). Gladwin explains that the group's artistic ways of working with headphones evolved from pragmatic solutions to unconventional site-specific spaces as it sought to fulfil the intention to '"empower the actors"' (quoted in Machon 2013: 171). The conversation and its mode of delivery through headphones manifest physical closeness to spectators so that the encounter seemed intimate as well as familiar as it diverted attention from preconceived ideas about disability.

Back to Back's brilliant 2019 production, *The Shadow Whose Prey the Hunter Becomes* directed by Gladwin, progressively moved to confronting the audience with a future reality of artificial intelligence (AI) determining all aspects of life so that so-called normal people are placed at an intellectual disadvantage. I viewed this production, 10 October 2019, at the Victorian Arts Centre, Melbourne. Set in a meeting hall, Scott (Price), Michael (Chan), Mark (Deans) and Sarah (Mainwaring) discussed who should speak and on behalf of whom given their diversity; Mark did not speak. As they acknowledged Scott as the most skilled computer user of the group, he called on Siri and the performers discussed her status as a non-person and how their context determines whether they choose to use the term disabled. Scott described feeling shame as a person with a disability that becomes compounded because he feels shame for feeling shame, a doubled sense of shame. The production outlined the shocking abuse of people with a disability in workplaces such as factory farms and a convent laundry in a prelude to a discussion of future types of work and AI. As the performers pointed out, everyone will have 'to live with the fear of being wrong'. The final declaration was made directly to the audience that in comparison with AI, 'you're going to have an intellectual disability' in the future. These productions invite recognition of the agency of individual performers as artists as part of an empathetic response.

For all its benefit, there are reservations about how empathy works in artistic processes. An empathetic response is not guaranteed and Graham McFee (2011) explains that imagining what it is like to be someone else might carry over into responses to others, but major differences in life experience make it difficult to empathize with, for example, a literary character in a different time and culture. Noel Carroll (2011) writes that fictional characters engage readers/spectators in asymmetry and within a broad 'appropriate resonance' rather than one narrowed to sympathetic or empathetic responses. Goldie (2011) writes that while he is not against imagining in 'perspective-shifting' what it would be like to be in the circumstances of someone else, he does have serious concerns about the empathetic imagining of literally being that person in real life (2011: 302–4). This suggests dual aspects of the function of empathy: one within a predetermined pattern and the other encouraging an open-ended process. Goldie is against the outcome that forestalls, even obliterates the agency of the other person, as happens with a predetermined pattern. Although both types involve imagination even pretence, Goldie distinguishes between empathy, which is potentially a positive engagement, and empathy as a substitution. The problem with substitution is that a person who empathetically imagines how the other person feels operates from a personal logic that presumes a comparable one in the other person, and within a psychological framework of projected emotional feelings. The presumption of knowing what another thinks and feels is what Goldie is questioning because the engagement is limited by one's own capacities.

A further question about empathy concerns the extent to which empathy encourages social activity on behalf of others. This is particularly relevant for empathy in support of campaigns for social justice, and this process needs to be larger than the person-to-person centred empathy. But the way in which empathy works might depend on an initial individual engagement in order to develop an appreciation for the predicament of a larger number. It may need social leadership to galvanize responses.

The capacity of empathy in representation more broadly is debated. While there is recognition of how events and their images impact on feelings in the public sphere and create 'normative modes', these often encourage fantasies of a good life that mask a different reality (Berlant 2011: 3). At the same time, contemporary mediated culture is saturated with violent imagery, which raises the concern that such exposure induces avoidance rather than empathetic action to redress wrongs. E. Ann Kaplan writes of the difficulty of facilitating ways for audiences to get beyond what is deemed either 'vicarious trauma' that induces immobilizing shock or a type of 'empty empathy' that makes spectators passive and engenders hopelessness (2011: 258, 264). The impact is unmistakably emotional. Kaplan explains, 'Traumatic images are the site where feelings become public' (2011: 276). In upholding concepts of witnessing, Kaplan argues for 'structures within which often silently endured traumatic experiences can be "spoken" or imagined' in order for people to engage empathetically and come together collectively to work against such injustice (2011: 276).

Theatrical performance potentially fulfils this purpose through its structure and artistic approaches and, because it is less direct than photographic media, it facilitates the sustained engagement conducive to empathetic feeling for diverse identities in complex circumstances. At the same time performance encourages self-reflection about felt responses.

Suffering in Jane Harrison's *Stolen*

Theatrical performance offers an important form of cultural communication because of an artistic capacity to elicit empathy through the personification of prejudice and suffering. The public expression of the emotional anguish of trauma in performance supports a social purpose to bear witness (Duggan 2012). This process is apparent with the re-enactment of colonization and dramatic stories about the suffering of First Nations Indigenous peoples (Burelle 2014). Jill Carter explains, however, that effective political performance must garner more than sympathy and evoke empathy to distinguish 'feeling *for* from feeling *with*' so as to recognize the individual agency of those who have suffered, and generate collaborative processes for political redress (2015: 424, italics in original). Empathetic social change needs to be determined by those from the marginalized community. Carter is analysing Canada's national responses leading up to the 2015 Final Report on Residential Schools by the Truth and Reconciliation Commission. She argues that sympathy might have a cathartic effect through outrage and guilt but it remains ineffectual and that public mourning needs to facilitate ongoing exchange between settler and Canadian Indian cultures.

The play, *Stolen*, by Australian Aboriginal playwright, Jane Harrison (1998), depicts the lasting impact of land dispossession, injustice and racist treatment in the lives of First Nations Australian Aboriginal people. The play's characters are assured of empathetic responses from readers/audiences and also respect for their courage and dignified endurance. In *Stolen*, Harrison depicts how Australian Aboriginal children were forcibly removed from their families until the 1970s in accordance with official government policy and placed in institutions or private homes. Although the play is based on research interviews with people who have become known in Australia as the 'Stolen Generation', it is not verbatim theatre staging the interview material and instead presents artistically crafted composite identities. Five performers enact five child characters as well as numerous other characters including the mothers of the children, other relatives and the offstage voices of authority. Harrison's play in production has been widely praised and it became one of Australia's biggest selling plays; *Stolen* encapsulates contemporary tragedy on a national scale.

The play's stories invite the reader/spectator to bear witness to the suffering of the recent past and the legacies of children abruptly taken from loving mothers. The 'stolen' children cry to go home. The play depicts five dormitory beds in a children's home, and these become a bedroom, a prison cell and an institution for the mentally ill, as *Stolen* progressively reveals what becomes of the children as adults. Importantly, the play explicitly outlines what happens emotionally to the characters through loss of family and the brutality of institutional lives (Harrison 1998: iii). Ruby believes that she has been abandoned by her family and, as a young woman, she is sexually and physically abused to the point where she breaks down. A member of the Stolen Generation herself, Shirley has her children taken from her and she desperately searches for them throughout her life. Young Anne is adopted and does not remember what happened; when she realizes, she becomes bewildered and ambivalent. Jimmy is described as being mischievous as a boy, shamed as an older boy, then angry as an adult who finally cannot withstand the torment, and not finding his family, he hangs himself in prison. This references the comparatively high number of Aboriginal people in gaol and a distressingly high number of deaths while in police custody. Sandy, who recounts the traditional stories told to him by his uncle, finds it difficult to settle anywhere but eventually finds a place to call home and develops what is called a 'sense of country' within Aboriginal culture.

The characters all suffer trauma in their lives and the consequences include mental illness, although these traumatic events are dramatically stylized. Performance need not stage trauma that might re-traumatize, while still continuing to have a visceral impact (Duggan 2012: 124–5). Jimmy's continuing incarceration destroys his life and any chance of emotional equilibrium, while Ruby manifests her suffering in emotional breakdown. In the scene 'Ruby's Descent into Madness', she is scrubbing the floor as the voices of others can be heard attacking, accusing and racially vilifying her until she screams 'Where are you?' and falls down, rocking (Harrison 1998: 27). The play's depictions counteract an idea that mental illness is attributable to individual pathologies in isolation from social factors. Instead character stories reinforce how the social circumstances of emotional and physical abuse have lifelong consequences for mental health. *Stolen* expressly exposes the immeasurable damage of the insidious crime of child sexual abuse.

The loss of Aboriginal knowledge going back over 60,000 years is conveyed but in a way that makes its legacy redemptive when Sandy recounts creation myths to the other children. He draws on the Aboriginal Dreamtime about the sun (*yurringa*), and the kangaroo (*barra*) on the hot earth, and how the Mungee or outcast has morphed into a monster with pale skin who is 'stealing our babies' (Harrison 1998: 11). The children enact the movement of hunting and take pride in the myths that point to traditional knowledge about managing the environment in sustainable ways. More light-hearted segments with children's games are interspersed with descriptions of racist treatment and crimes: 'being treated like a dog' and called one; and being forced to become servants, cleaning and cooking for white families (Harrison 1998: 15, 26). The horror of life in the children's home emerges from matter-of-fact depictions alongside the tragedy of the constant efforts of the mothers to find their children and communicate with letters (Hughes 2015). These letters were never received and only discovered by the adult children when they try to find their families, and often tragically after a mother has died. Shirley describes how it rained when, without a word to her, 'they' took her son, as she stood unable to move before finally falling down (Harrison 1998: 9). Reading this brief speech evokes an empathetic response to the grief of this mother.

As *Stolen* presents traumatic events, its composite storytelling invites empathetic responses from reader/spectators. In this way, as Coplan argues, empathy leads to 'experiential understanding' which deepens cognition (2011: 17). She outlines an enlarged process of understanding that exceeds a narrative of cause and effect, and encourages taking responsibility.

Written and workshopped over six years, *Stolen* was first produced by Ilbijerri Aboriginal and Torres Strait Islander Theatre Co-operative in 1998 with well-known director, Wesley Enoch, working with an experienced cast of Aboriginal actors and artists. The play's form intersperses short, realist dialogue that shifts backwards and forwards in time, with nonrealist elements – Enoch's production used photographic images and puppets. The capacity of images to evoke compassion is recognized as contributing to the struggle for social change (Lydon 2016). The production framed the suffering of what happened to Aboriginal people within the consequences of intergenerational trauma, and the struggles against racist attitudes that continue. As Maryrose Casey explains, although the play was being developed from 1992, *Stolen* was welcomed by many Australians and internationally in the context of the 1997 *Bringing Them Home* report about the stolen generation and public demonstrations for official reconciliation between Aboriginal and white settler cultures, culminating in 2000 with Australia's largest march of 250,000 people walking across the Sydney Harbour Bridge (Casey 2004: 208–10). In 2008, the then Prime Minister, Kevin Rudd, delivered an apology to the Stolen Generations on behalf of the Australian people and government.

The theatrical performance discussed here confirms the function of empathy but also its complexities. The theoretical discussion of empathy makes a distinction between recognizing the thoughts and feelings of another and being able to experience what is being felt, although it presumes aspects of both. But readers/spectators of *Stolen* would not necessarily have a comparable experience and are responding to the artistic effect. Alvin Goldman suggests that two 'routes' to empathy are offered through the development of neurological mirroring and through 'reconstructive' enactment and imagining, and it is possible that one underlies the other (2011: 41, 44). Science confirms physiological reactions, but these acquire a more complex capacity through forms of cultural communication. The proposition that layered routes to empathy may be what matters aligns with how performances simultaneously evoke thought, affect and emotional feeling often summarized as empathy in spectator responses. Creatively imagined theatrical practice personifies and embodies suffering within a multi-layered mix of familiar and unfamiliar experiences. Audience groups witness stories of injustice which consolidate empathetic responses to suffering.

Theatrical performance itself becomes a type of social action. In an examination of what empathy is doing, Lindsay Cummings (2016) proposes that the exchange between social concern and theatre and performance pivots on empathy and generates a public dialogue. It can be effective in depicting suffering in war and people seeking asylum to illuminate what is felt and thought (e.g. Grehan 2009; Cummings 2016). Patrick Duggan investigates what he calls types of '*trauma-tragedy*' across drama and contemporary live arts, and he finds that it is almost a subgenre, and it includes autobiographical suffering in which he theorizes that trauma-symptoms necessitate re-enactment by the sufferer, and which co-opts performance (2012: 7, italics in original). Duggan links empathetic responses to kinaesthetic ones in a whole body experience as he describes performances that range from those that restage stories of political trauma to embodied physical acts without an explicit context (2012: 110). Theatrical depictions of trauma may be important for reinforcing somatic processes of empathy (Blair 2009); these expand through the repetition of such engagement over time.

Social processes for empathy include the theatrical and other types of performance that compound and create multi-layered experiences of empathetic engagement within cultural communication. But performance implicates bodily processes in the transformation of personal responses into socially responsible values conducive to collaborative action. Significantly, the performance of suffering supports embodied political action.

Feeling sound and images: Robert Lepage's *Needles and Opium* and *887*

The concluding case study of Section Two analyses the visually imaginative political performance of performer-director Robert Lepage that combines fictional and real identities, and impersonal technologies and personal narratives, to create a balanced evocation of affect, emotional feeling and empathy. Based in Canada, Lepage creates characters and personae who are often coming to terms with the impositions of language, place and identity within political contexts that are multilingual and intercultural. Lepage's capacity to enhance a spoken narrative with complex multimedia and filmed footage denotes live performance for an increasingly image-dominated twenty-first-century society. A combination of locations and intersecting narratives communicates with audiences in accessible ways (Dundjerovic 2009: 47–9; Harvie 2000). Lepage's performance depicting subjective identity can seem quite intimate yet contain multiple strands as the visual action enlarges the storytelling.

Emotional tones of sadness and melancholy seep through the staging, noticeably in stories about thwarted love, longing and anguish encompassing same-sex relationships. Although melancholy can be challenging to convey in performance, Lepage manages to illuminate moments of this evocative poetic quality in the aesthetic effects and in theatrical stories of love.

Lepage's performance points to melancholy associated with LGBTQI experience and destabilized gender identity. In Freud's extended description of mourning and melancholia, the latter's somatic experience encompasses 'self-reproaches' and 'self-revilings' (1914–16: 244). In writing about Freud's concepts, Butler explains that what has been lost and mourned is clear, whereas melancholia is about 'not knowing' and they converge in 'losing what we cannot fully fathom' (2004b: 22). Melancholia suggests felt experience that is elusive and abstruse.

Emotional effects such as poetic melancholy in Lepage's productions emerge from the combined artistic effect. Lepage is lucidly forthright about the function of emotions in performance and he disapproves of performers acting emotional feeling in comments recorded in Michel Duchesne's documentary *The 7 Faces of Robert Lepage*. It shows how Lepage collaborates with an artistic team, and the performers, in a creative development process inclusive of visual design, so that, in jest, Lepage calls himself a 'traffic director' of artists. They, in turn, acknowledge his highly imaginative capacity and use of objects. Lepage argues that artists need to respect the intelligence of their audiences who come together randomly, and 'it's not merely communication but a sort of communion' created with the audience (*The 7 Faces of Robert Lepage* 1997). Lepage is critical of the trend for actors to emote a sequence of emotional feelings, in that trying hard to express these becomes counterproductive because it 'rarely – if ever – reaches the audience' (*The 7 Faces of Robert Lepage* 1997). Instead he expects the feelings to be those of the audience. As well, Lepage clearly states that performance should never be therapy for artists – like himself. His work resists overt expressions of emotion and his comments suggest that emotional feeling is an indirect effect of the theatrical performance. Performers should avoid showing audiences what to feel, so emotional feeling, empathy and affective sensation arise through connecting with the whole performance.

Needles and Opium was first created by Robert Lepage in 1991 as a solo show, and it brought international recognition. One memorable image evoking affect involved Lepage suspended off the ground against a filmed projection of a moving spiral; it was metaphoric of suspended cultural identity. Although the central persona in the performance is called Robert, it can be staged without Lepage, and in 2013 he directed Marc Labrèche to play Robert in the remounted touring version with multiple cast members. It was described by Robert Crew as a 'masterpiece' in a newer, theatrically reconfigured production (2013: E.2). *Needles and Opium* presented three intersecting biographical narratives of artists and unconventional love affairs (Bunzli 2000). Contrasting two time periods and countries, *Needles and Opium* featured the great African-American jazz musician, Miles Davis, in Paris in 1949 and in love with Frenchwoman, Juliette Gréco; the bisexual French writer and auteur, Jean Cocteau, returning from New York; and a narrator artist called Robert in the United States, who has been left by his male lover in the 1980s. The artist of the narrative was doubled by the artist performer (Lepage or Labrèche). *Needles and Opium* linked the loss of an intense love with the withdrawal from an addictive drug, and the spaces associated with travel, mobility, dreams and hallucinations suggested fantasy and altered reality (Dundjerovic 2009: 45, 50). Concepts of love and creativity were central, as they are in Lepage's later works.

Gréco is on the public record about her love affair with Davis in response to a question from philosopher, Jean-Paul Sartre, about why they did not marry. She states that Davis loved her too much to want her to be unhappy. Davis foresaw that an interracial marriage would be rejected in the United States at that time. *Needles and Opium* implicitly contrasted obstacles to romantic union historically including the social rejection of homosexual relationships so that ideas about the lack of freedom to choose who to love were delicately woven into the visual and aural presentation. *Needles and Opium* charted the psychological consequences of nonconformity to identity norms and invited empathy for those who have been socially rejected, and as covert relationships became fraught with guilt and fear. It revealed a political significance to intimate emotional suffering. The flux of melancholic feeling exposed the consequences of socially prescriptive relationships.

Lepage specifies it is '"the sound that does the work"' and with careful selection of music and to avoid explaining the meaning (Defraeye 2000: 81) (also see Section Three). The theatrical modes of *Needles and Opium* and including Davis's music became associated with a melancholic sadness alongside narratives of unattainable love. The music and the images worked together and generated an impression of other-worldliness in its mood and to expose how cultural memory and personal memory intersect. Aleksandar Dundjerovic elaborates on the influence of Cocteau's ideas of art and his film, *Orphée*, on Lepage's artistic approach and use of poetic and mythic elements (2009: 49). A setting in *Needles and Opium* that seemed familiar acquired a quality of strangeness as the staging unfolded and its unsettling mood effect could linger and influence perceptions of what followed.

All the while the evocation of emotional feeling contributes to perceptions of identity in theatrical performance since gender can be intentionally destabilized by overturning norms of emotional display or suppression. Hence emotional display can feminize (male) identity and create a queer effect. In considering queer identity, Butler writes about suffering and the melancholia of suppressed mourning due to 'a prohibition on certain forms of love' (2004a: 199). A melancholic dimension to queer love stories reveals subjective as well as socially structured feeling: the torment of queerness. A haunting melancholic impression in Lepage's performance conveys how thwarted love, longing and loss disrupt the self.

James Bunzli (2000) describes a notion of the self that is fragmented and refracted in Lepage's solo work. Commenting on his productions with other performers, Josette Féral explains that Lepage's characters 'narrate themselves' often while travelling and, in this way, he explores an idea of becoming self and as if seeking an authentic entity (2009: 148). Characters in Lepage's performance search for who they might be – the self needs to be discovered. This seems familiar to audiences because the performance replicates how people tell a personal story to others and thereby establish a sense of self through its repetition. A search for self-knowledge parallels the explorative processes of creation fundamental to art. In Lepage productions, the parallel life stories span history, memory and other cultures and, in their telling, echo a process of remembering and recounting significant events in combination with tangential small details that coalesce into what seems like a personal story.

Lepage's theatrical productions might or might not start with a written script although his initial directing is called a process of 'writing' (quoted in Dundjerovic 2009: 24). New works take longer to stage and Lepage is criticized for this, but he emphasizes collaboration, and the first production of a work is still a work in progress (Dundjerovic 2009: 30–1). He offers public rehearsals to find out what is working for audiences. Lepage's productions include plural languages and countries, physical action and ideas as he works across both live art and film to stir the affect, emotional feeling and empathy of audiences.

As a director, Lepage's approach is dramatically visual and therefore effective in film and in circus where the visual action provides the crucial component. Lepage's cross-arts work includes directing the Cirque du Soleil productions of *KÀ* for a purpose-built Las Vegas venue that opened in 2005 and *Totem,* Cirque's touring tent show that opened in 2010 (Leroux and Batson 2016). Both Lepage and Cirque have expanded the artistic boundaries of technology in performance in pursuit of imaginative aesthetic environments with affective impact. Cirque's narratives in nonverbal physical performance are far less detailed than Lepage's theatrical storytelling of love and sexuality, but the muscular female and graceful male ambiguously gendered bodies in the early 1990s Cirque shows were culturally significant for mainstream audiences. The bodily sensation of watching circus movement and fast acrobatic action might be more apparent, but a comparable, if more subtle, affect can also be discerned within Lepage's theatrical performance.

In a thorough explanation of sight and other sensory perception in performance, Stephen Di Benedetto describes the physiological functions of the body and brain and the limbic system, and explains that some consciousness of the accompanying bodily sensations is achieved through 'constant monitoring over time', but that such an effect is individually moderated (2010: 7). Connections between the senses, language and memory are unmistakable because these functions converge in the cerebrum of the brain, which additionally shapes imagination and sorts sensory information and, importantly, distinguishes emotional feelings (Di Benedetto 2010: 3; Payne 2014). The senses appear to function together, but Di Benedetto explains that different types of performance can increase awareness of one sense through, for example, theatrical lighting or sound. The affects of engagement can be illuminated where performance delivers strong sensory elements, in ways that also encourage awareness of responses. Theatrical innovation especially encourages the (sense) memory of a performance.

887 was a performance about memory that evoked affect, emotional feeling and empathy in relation to memory's embodied functions. It innovatively interwove the subject self of a narrator named Robert into a larger political context, and Lepage drew directly on his own life. *887* juxtaposed Lepage's childhood life in an apartment building at 887 Avenue Murray in Quebec City with his current adult life. This solo performance by Lepage explored how personal life and political events intersect in memory as it reflected on theatrical memorization and the physiological failure of memory.

I found myself surprised that the sensory impact of Lepage's 2015 performance, *887*, could be so wondrous; I saw the performance at the Victorian Arts Centre in Melbourne on 20 October 2016. Lepage worked within a beautifully designed set that conveyed childhood wonder and, like Mabou Mine's *Dollhouse*, contained a contrasting scale so the performer was larger than the set which elicited affect. But I was emotionally moved at the show's end although I could not exactly explain how this was achieved as there was no noticeable display of facial and embodied expression. It could be feasibly attributed to Lepage's signature elements, so that the emotional feelings were not explained and expressed but emerged indirectly from the combined theatrical effects including the background music and sound.

The past was indicated by a beautifully designed, miniaturized apartment building. In the present, Robert received an invitation to commemorate events of 1970 by delivering the poem, 'Speak White', by Québécois writer Michèle Lalonde (n.d.), which was once a symbol of radical ethnic and economic protest. The poem highlighted the colloquial insult contained in its title of advocating the upholding of English language and white cultural traditions from the past, and a line claimed 'liberty' as a black word. The memory of Robert's family life in 1970 was set against the campaign by Quebec's separatist movement (FLQ) for political recognition of language-based ethnic identity, and in the context of economic disadvantage and class struggle. The ensuing terrorist acts by the FLQ were presented in their historical specificity; yet, this implicitly pointed to trying to understand recent acts of terrorism. *887* depicted 4,000 police with truncheons against 680 demonstrators demanding political autonomy. The past and the present were additionally linked to the future by a narrative thread about a longstanding friend of Robert who revealed that, in his work as an announcer, he had voiced Robert's 'cold cut' – his death notice – for the Canadian Broadcasting Corporation (CBC). Robert was shocked that his thirty-five years of theatrical work was to be remembered in a perfunctory way. Culture's processes of remembering can also distort what happened and what has been achieved.

Lepage performed in a rotating set stepping into his kitchen in the present and standing outside the exterior of the family's apartment at 887 and a 1960s diner. As Robert described his family's apartment, a model of the whole building appeared on stage alongside him to enchant, its height matching his. He bent down to peer into the six floors of apartments as he described the inhabitants in nostalgic reflection. Some were represented by filmed footage projected on to a segment of the model building and others by small, doll-like figures. The sadness of the musician playing Chopin in the downstairs apartment who had been injured in a car accident that killed his fiancée was juxtaposed with the humour of a two-timing female concierge and the fascination for a couple upstairs who fought and argued constantly. Robert idealized his French-speaking, taxi-driving, emotionally distant father. As the narrative progressed, Robert's grandmother came to live in the crowded apartment. The family and father's care of the grandmother who suffered memory loss from Alzheimer's disease invited an empathetic response and to a dilemma familiar to many in the audience since the father would not let her be put into a residential home. In Robert's childhood world, his grandmother's extreme emotions, her tears and rage, were part of her deteriorating brain condition. She embodied a loss of self with her loss of memory and emotional control. Robert mentioned 'visceral memory', the bodily sensation of memory, and, back in his kitchen in the present, struggled to memorize lines.

While the spoken text moved between realist narration and poetic refrain, the changing visual text became like an emotionally evocative companion, and the building proportioned to human height required sensory adjustment, which made its affect noticeable. Further adjustment was required as the set changed scale when Lepage was overshadowed by a television and chair. Robert described the colonial history and remembered the FLQ bombs and a serial killer around the time that Queen Elizabeth II visited Canada, touring in a Lincoln car named after the American president. A toy size Lincoln car, a prop, symbolized the intertwined personal and political events as Robert remembered the excitement of a boyhood Christmas gift and observed, pointedly, that President de Gaulle from France toured in a Lincoln. The car acquired winsome qualities as the object of personal, political and cultural memories.

Crucially, both affect and emotional feeling were described in *887*. The boy Robert came under the 'spell' of Chopin. The text explained how musical notes spark the spatial memory of the brain and stimulate the hippocampus. The affective dimensions of sound were made explicit with a diagram of the brain looking down from above, and it showed the brain's divided hemispheres with the left side being logical and right side being emotional. This is transferred into the two sides of the apartment building, with the right side prone to domestic disputes. While sadness is associated with the brain's right hemisphere, joy and affection are more likely to correlate with the left, but this allocation only provides an imprecise guideline, because the brain is flexible and changeable. The production was gently nostalgic for family life, pragmatically revealing about Canadian politics, and evocatively empathetic in its depiction of the loneliness of Robert's mother, and the grief of Robert's father over his mother. What went unsaid was Robert's grief for his father.

Robert went to see performers at the conservatorium where he trained at a time when university was largely taxpayer funded in Canada. His former teacher pointed out that only those with the economic resources to pay could do the actor training course in the twenty-first century. The students were performing *The Birds* by Aristophanes (1969), an infrequently performed comedy about a city of birds convinced by two humans to go to war with the gods. Its inclusion seemed significant because *The Birds* parodies hypocritical practices in which birds symbolize love and provide omens in religious practices while being trapped, traded and consumed as food. It lends itself to contemporary interpretation about contradictory emotional attitudes towards other animal species and a growing commitment to veganism among young people who are adopting ethical attitudes towards the environment shared with other species. *887* contrasted cultural memory about twentieth-century political action with a glimpse of twenty-first-century political activism.

The ending of *887* was a mimed sequence. A spectator saw only the taxi's headlights and top light, and the silhouette of the driver. If the production's evocation of affect came from sensory responses to the aural, physical and visual staging with its designed contrasts in scale, at the end, the performance conveyed an undercurrent of sadness. While *887* may not have had this impact on other audience members, and those around me were asking what 'Speak White' meant for race politics, puzzlement involving thought can be considered an affect.

I responded with empathetic melancholic feeling at the end. Since Lepage's delivery was understated and recounted events in a matter-of-fact tone, perhaps it was the narrative that had an emotional impact – as Aristotle proposes. But the final scene was the culmination of preceding episodes of subtle moments of remembrance about people now dead suggesting grief, and the performance text also equated remembered spaces of culture with loss. The capacity to draw out melancholic sadness as the final impression was the culmination of textual distillation and captivating visual imagery, in a whole-of-production effect. While melancholy confirmed a poetic aesthetic, it aligned with the emotional sensibilities of a performative self.

The dynamics of this production made it emotionally compelling in one part, and enjoyable and thought provoking in others. If I responded with affect in the immediate moment of the visual staging and with empathy for the family caring for the grandmother, an emotional impression was apparent in the final part, and the melancholic mood lingered afterwards. The mood of *887* gradually shifted from enchanting engagement to sadness.

As outlined throughout this section, realist and nonrealist genres can induce affect and/or emotional feeling and empathy at different points and in contrasting ways during a performance. These emerge from the subtle layered shifts in visual and verbal effects; in intangible effects that twist and turn, performance sets itself apart from the everyday. As it bears witness to personal suffering and persecution in life, affect and empathy evocation in the multi-dimensional effects of a collaborative art form have the potential to illuminate aspects of human experience in profound ways. The experience of being in an audience compounds this affective and emotional capacity and accumulates within the mood of performance.

SECTION THREE

Mood and case studies

This section considers how the aesthetic mood in performance contributes to the impact and the significance of theatrical genres from the enjoyable big budget production to the confronting one-to-one performance. While comparatively harder to explain than the emotions, aesthetic mood incites an individual spectator's emotional mood and potentially reflects a social mood about events in the world. An exploration of mood in performance thereby reveals connections to ideological belief and economic values.

The case studies discussed below illuminate the ways in which performance creates an immersive mood from the 'feel-good' and uplifting effects of large-scale musicals such as *The Lion King* and *Dear Evan Hansen* to the ominous moods of Socìetas Raffaello Sanzio productions reflecting the emotional intensity of Artaud's 'theatre of cruelty'. Similarly, the experience of live art such as *The Artist Is Present* by Marina Abramovic involves an intimate exchange that confronts and intimidates.

Debates about the function of music coincide with how theatrical mood straddles the physiology of feeling and the cultural evocation of the emotions and emotional feelings. Physiology and mood music intersected in Rimini Protokoll's *Brain Projects* about brains and their study. Furthermore, workers taught intonation and expression for emotional feelings under neoliberalist politics and globalization in *Alladeen*, directed by Marianne Weems, exposed mood disorders and anger within the prevailing economic order. By removing emotional intonation from speech, The Wooster Group's *To You, the Birdie! (Phèdre)* objectified emotional feeling for audience scrutiny and devolved theatrical responsibility for mood. While theatre's fearful eco-moods point to a dystopian near-future, the promise of sensory collaborative processes anticipates happier shared moods.

Mysterious aesthetic

An exploration of aesthetic mood needs to consider its emotional scope, especially since artistic mood is commonly associated with an impression of melancholic longing. When the Russian director Vsevolod Meyerhold writes of the 'theatre of mood' in opposition to naturalistic realism in 1906, he advocates that theatrical artistry captures sparse poetic effects, claiming that 'the spectator's imagination is able to supply that which is left unsaid' so that theatre creates a mystery which compels spectators to want to 'solve it' (1969: 25). They puzzle over mood. He rejects productions that provide the audience with every visual and aural detail in preference for a theatre with qualities that are inconclusive – like mood. But Meyerhold understands that this is an artistic effect and he points out that 'the secret of Chekhov's mood lies in the *rhythm* of his language' (1969: 32, italics in original). Poetic language can create mood effects in literature and in theatrical performance with heightened and condensed phrasing. Even though Meyerhold seeks a sense of mystery through visual theatre, his example suggests how mood effects can be achieved even in poetic realism.

Although mood commonly indicates an individual's recognizable, if not necessarily controllable, emotional experience, mood in theatrical performance is artistically created through its aesthetic elements. Artistic mood connects with individual experience when literature, cinema and performance invite engagement with, even immersion in, an imagined world. Mood is less specific than an emotion and thus can be described with a range of words. It differs from the numerous emotional interactions and declarations between characters and can be distinguished further from affect because of its deliberate creation. While theatrical emotions are strongly intentional, a mood is less purposeful and more reliant on spectator imagination.

The consideration of mood brings to the fore sensory responses within the performance environment, itself recognized as offering 'atmospheres' and especially through the use of multimedia (Eckersall, Grehan and Scheer 2017). Atmosphere is being used in relation to affect, which is less contained whereas an immersive mood also connects with emotional impact during performance. Both mood and atmosphere highlight processes of seeing and listening and in the body's rapidly shifting sensory interactions. In arguing for the recognition of sensory modes of interpretation and the '*performative power of the senses*', André Lepecki and Sally Banes explain that making and perceiving performance involve removing the conceptual 'boundaries of the visually iconic and of the linguistically and musically sonic' because oscillating 'vestibular and kinesthetic senses' are fundamental (2007: 3, italics in original). Interestingly, they point out that the emphasis on one particular sense, such as sight over sound, can shift once cultural difference and preference for sound over sight are taken into account. Aesthetic mood connects with the kinaesthetic exchange that compounds the sensory perception of theatrical performance.

Audience expectations and
The Lion King

Researchers in psychology demonstrate that a subject's mood can be changed by watching a happy or a sad film to induce a comparable mood (Clore and Gasper 2000: 12). In an example from live performance, the continuing popularity of large-scale musicals in the twenty-first century demonstrates the wide appeal of what is colloquially termed a 'feel-good' experience. Audiences expect to enjoy a performance of cheerful exhilaration because it cultivates a happy mood (Hurley 2010: 22). But sizeable casts and spectacular staging can be expensive to mount, so there can be a direct connection between a 'feel-good' impression and the cost of a production, including the cost of extensive marketing to attract audiences. For example, one of the most successful Broadway musicals, *The Lion King*, reportedly cost $10–12 million to mount in 1997 (Sternfeld 2006: 322), and *Wicked* reputedly cost $20 million a decade later. Granted, there can be considerable financial return from the investment if a production continues over years and an expensive large-scale production can be relied on for its 'feel-good' appeal. Such an effect can also be achieved with a small budget production albeit for a much smaller audience.

Musical theatre can be analysed for a plethora of cultural meaning, and Millie Taylor (2012) finds political meaning in its pleasures. Stacy Wolf (2011) discerns political punch and power in the emotional dynamics of the Broadway musical. Emotional effects contribute to the esteem, meaning and economic value of a production. While a successful production relies on the capacity of creative teams, it frequently adheres to an established format for the structure, character, music and action – one known to be effective. Even an unexpected hit musical such as Jonathan Larson's *Rent*, that started as a low-budget production with atypical character types and depictions of urban street life, drug addiction, homosexuality, homelessness and violence, retained the conventional structural elements of music theatre as well as elements from the popular opera, Puccini's *La Bohème* (Sternfeld 2006: 325–8). This is comparable to how a film genre delivers emotion within a predetermined range; for example, the mood of a romantic comedy progresses towards a happy or at least a positive resolution for the characters so that obstacles and upsets are temporary interludes. There is a calculated effort to the emotional mood that contributes to the appeal of commercially successful performance.

While artistic novelty might please and surprise audiences, some of the success of large-scale productions can be attributed to external factors such as habits of attendance and social preferences. In an era of growing economic volatility and political insecurity, a celebratory, uplifting mood in performance might appeal for its diversionary effect. Social circumstances are temporarily left behind.

The live musical of *The Lion King* was developed from the animated Disney film, an early indication of a twenty-first-century trend to remake a successful film into a live stage show. It appealed to a wide audience and particularly families, and the esteemed adaptation became one of the longest running stage shows in London, New York and other major cities around the world. *The Lion King*'s theatrical articulation of the animal kingdom presented a coming-of-age story set in Africa with a young male lion, Simba, learning about life and morality, initially in a father–son dynamic and then in a Hamlet-like contest with a malevolent uncle in preparation for Simba's future as king. With the exception of one wise Zulu woman, the characters in the live production were singing and speaking animals and birds. The overall mood was upbeat, effervescent and buoyant, and Simba's struggles endearing. Set to music and lyrics by Elton John and Tim Rice, the live production was innovatively directed by Julie Taymor and, in collaboration with other artists, Taymor created highly original, beautiful puppets and masks. The production's familial sentiments and heart-warming emotions were characterized by animal identities and framed by stirring music, emotionally familiar narratives and music forms, and fantastic visual design.

The 'feel-good' effect of this type of stage show came from immersion in an imaginative theatrical world. The dynamic mood from music and movement and combined technical effects could seem wonderful. A deliberate intention to please if not amaze with such a performance revealed how a concept such as wonder can be aligned with an aesthetic mood. Wonder offers an example of how mood differs from an emotional feeling since wonder is comprehended – the feeling of wonder is sometimes termed an 'affect'. Wonder is recognized rather than emotionally felt as 'raw sensation' and therefore can be categorized as a mood (Felski and Fraiman 2012: viii).

The promise of a happier mood from attendance at a large-scale musical implicates ideas of happiness and consumption in the build-up to the performance and the after effect. In her analysis of its inherent contradictions, Sara Ahmed (2010) finds that happiness is not so much reliant on a purchase or a possession that can be obtained or participation in an event, but a pursuit. Therefore, she argues, happiness is not itself an object that can be possessed, although contradictorily material objects often symbolize the pursuit of happiness. In an interesting parallel, consideration of emotion in economic theory is exemplified by longstanding discourse about happiness. Luigino Bruni and Pier Luigi Porta (2005) summarize debates since the 1970s describing 'the paradox of happiness' in which striving for and obtaining higher income do not correlate with a corresponding rise in levels of happiness once there is sufficient income to meet actual need as it is determined within each society. While a mistaken belief encourages continued striving for economic gain, individual happiness is determined by a far more complex set of nature and nurture influences, and closely aligned with a sense of control in life. Significantly, the idea of happiness is replaced in its study with concepts such as 'satisfaction', 'purpose' and 'flourishing' through activity and to align with measures of wellbeing (Nussbaum 2005: 171). Happiness translates into a 'feel-good' or uplifting mood effect in the performance example of *The Lion King*. This type of substitution becomes necessary because happiness remains a subjective experience of psychological mood, and thus it is difficult to quantify and to compare between individuals, and because happiness seems unstable – fluctuating daily and across a lifetime. This process of using substitute concepts remains relevant to theatre practitioners and typifies how aesthetic mood is conceived.

The Lion King might have charmed audiences but the enchanting mood was also emotionally misleading. The mood effect relied on an unquestioning acceptance of the theatrical pretence and its moral predicament, so that unqualified enjoyment of the production might have been contingent on a spectator's background and values. The cultural sensitivities and political implications of an imagined Africa in lieu of a large continent with diverse nations and geographies and specific racial, ethnic and national identities were, to some extent, offset in the live production by the use of six African languages and some ethnic diversity in casting. Real world concerns and racial hierarchies were deflected into an anthropocentric animal kingdom and through a process of emotional species substitution.

The emotional relationships in *The Lion King* were sentimentalized exchanges set within animal and geographical worlds of this highly imaginative production. Animal puppets and masks with visible human handlers enacted the narrative and the accompanying emotions, which were superimposed on animal character identities. Emotions also became associated with a stage object. At the same time this type of engagement reflected the longstanding function of animals in thought and in the representation of emotions (Ridout 2006; Tait 2012); in Western culture these practices go back to Aesop's fables originating in ancient Greece. Lions symbolized human family emotions in both the theatrical and cinematic languages of *The Lion King*, which additionally points to a process of childhood affection directed towards animals. Notwithstanding that free-roaming lions are declining in number due to habitat loss, this type of production instilled a false belief in cross-species emotional compatibility by overlaying human emotional relationships and moral dilemmas on to other animal species. An enchanting mood was created by a theatrical fantasy of 'feel-good' species relations.

Following Darwin's proposition that nonhuman animals have emotions like humans, twentieth-century evolutionary researchers recognized correspondences in aspects of behaviour and, more recently, comparable emotional feeling through attention to, and familiarity with, animal lives and facial expressions (de Waal 2009). But these are interpreted within human emotional understanding of the world, and humans can misinterpret nonhuman animal body language and facial reactions. The philosophical proposition that it is difficult to know the subjective feeling experience of another is magnified in relation to animal species. What an animal might feel emotionally remains conjecture. In addition, since the response threshold and intensity of emotional feeling differ between individual humans, these more than likely diverge between species. Granted, animal pets are socialized by human emotional communication. The way in which animals are expected to embody human emotions and contribute to a cheerful or fearful mood, however, relies on the mistaken belief that emotions are the same for everyone.

The aesthetic experience of the imaginative *The Lion King* was highly engaging – no doubt even for spectators such as myself with cognitive reservations about its African and animal concepts. It was difficult to resist being caught up in the emotional aesthetics and a prevailing mood of enjoyment. An opposite mood, however, can also attract audiences, and the capacity to willingly engage with so-called negative moods of sadness or even terror in theatre has been noted since Aristotle. Regardless, the aesthetic appeal relies on heightened mood effects in performance.

Ambiance from Socìetas Raffaello Sanzio

The strong images, inventive sound and sensory power of contemporary performance deliver an ambient mood effect that often has an enigmatic appeal. A mood of ominous threat hovered throughout Socìetas Raffaello Sanzio's *Tragedia Endogonidia* cycle, directed by Romeo Castellucci. The production presented a tragedy for the future consisting of eleven evolving parts that were staged in ten European cities and one American city between 2001 and 2005. The company's strongly visual productions, abstract soundscapes and elliptic content correspond with Meyerhold's idea of a mysterious 'theatre of mood'. *Tragedia Endogonidia*'s imagery was strongly biological as the human body was repeatedly placed with either an animal such as a goat, a cat, a chimpanzee or a machine or a vehicle or a robot. Internet segments included a naked woman seemingly with no face; chemical reactions against a naked man's skin; a figure on top of a car; a little person with an animal horn; a disembodied human face; and a female body disintegrating in front of the audience, the flesh dripping off the table. Castellucci collaborated with Scott Gibbons to create the unsettling soundscape that served this potent visual theatre and was crucial to its affect and emotional impact (Di Benedetto 2010: 164–5, 187–93). Stirring sentimental music cut across reassembled fragments of sound with variable pitch, speed and volume, and created eerie disturbance (Eckersall et al. 2017: 142). Pulsating, flapping and hissing nonhuman noises flowed into human ones, a child whispering, an operatic song. The overwhelming mood effect was a sense of foreboding and apprehension.

The company's performance explores tragic legacies within contemporary life. It bears witness to trauma and violence in society, past and present, with open-ended images (Grehan 2009; Duggan 2012: 66–75), which also means that there can be ambiguity in the ethical significance of the action and imagery. Significantly, Joe Kelleher discerns suffering conveyed through the tragic, often beautiful images (2004: 192). Productions have included dogs and horses on stage delivering strangeness and action that can shock and evoke visceral reactions to the enactment of attack and pain. Patrick Duggan discerns an 'unsteady mimesis' in the way that real world objects and living animals dominate so that realness seems to irrupt theatre's mimetic function (2012: 63–4). Adrian

Kear finds that spectator involvement in the immediacy of a production becomes like a '*co*-appearance' with the performer, for example, through a reference to (Dante's) inferno, the spectator became complicit in imagining a frightening world suggestive of hell (2013: 129, italics in original). Kear quotes Walter Benjamin to explain that the temporal convergences of Castellucci's productions seem to offer an 'extract of the future' (2013: 129).

Socìetas productions juxtapose moods of anguish and torment with calmness and moments of humour as they offer a twenty-first-century manifestation of Antonin Artaud's 'theatre of cruelty' with ritualistic rhythm and compelling dream-like contrasts of mythic elements and familiar objects. Castellucci's *Genesi* production included the recorded voice of Artaud calling out against God (Eckersall et al. 2017: 142). As he describes immersion in an intensely visceral 'theatre of cruelty' encompassing violent images, Artaud contends that an 'emotional athleticism' creates the intangible spaces of this theatre to engender fear and hallucinatory experience (1976: 215, 259). Artaud rejects realist theatre with its logical psychologies and emotional conflict replacing it with a contradictory theatre that stylizes and physicalizes states of mind and through gesture, and 'rhythm, the musical quality of physical movement' (1976: 216). He describes a spectacle of embodied signs and sounds and the music in ritualized Balinese performance which creates dense intangible experience with metaphysical impact – this may seem somewhat orientalist. Artaud describes 'mysterious fear' created by the 'emotional musculature' of the performer who becomes an 'athlete of the heart' performing emotionality as a physical discipline (Artaud 1976: 236, 259, 260). Artaud is attracted to the cruel shock induced by such performance.

The mood of Castellucci's productions evoked mysterious fear that remained after the performance ended (Di Benedetto 2010: 165). As Jonathan Flatley (2008) argues, it is the momentary effort to hold on to an experience of mood that denotes how artistically created mood becomes absorbed. The artistic capture of mood in literature and performance requires reader/spectator effort to prolong the immediate impact. Aesthetic mood manifests through a feeling for the mood. It might unfold through an effort to hold on to it or, alternatively, unstable qualities might be fleetingly glimpsed. An elusive dimension draws spectator attention as it constitutes the essence of aesthetic mood.

Music functions and Rimini Protokoll's *Brain Projects*

When performance uses music to support its aesthetic effect and movement, music and mood function together. Music may indeed inculcate mood as in 'feel-good' musicals but an explanation of how music achieves this effect for the listener is not straightforward. The impact of music without lyrics is interpreted as being achieved either through its accumulated cultural significance or through the sensory impact of the physical sound. This contrast overlaps with the issue of whether emotional feeling is stirred through either cognitive association or embodied responses. In her study of the arousal of emotion by music, Jenefer Robinson (2012) explains how wedding music, dance music and military music have become such an inseparable part of the social event, the music stands for that event. But there are debates about whether music induces emotional feeling in an individual in the moment or activates a pre-existing attunement. These debates mostly centre on music as a stand-alone art form, whereas music in theatrical performance has a context and it contributes to an overall aesthetic effect through its functions.

Robinson summarizes the functions of music as follows (2012: 654). Firstly, people associate significant personal situations with music so a love song carries emotional significance. Secondly, music contains aesthetic qualities that arouse admiration. Thirdly, the structure of a piece of music can unfold in ways that stir emotional responses. Fourthly, there might be qualities to the composition that convey to a listener what happens to someone experiencing an emotion such as sadness. Music and sound underscored the spoken text of the German-based Rimini Protokoll's *Brain Projects*, investigating how the brain works (Rimini Protokoll 2016). The aural composition by Barbara Morgenstern with Sven Janetzko corresponded with Robinson's delineated functions. A sober dignified musical score raised the mood out of the everyday and, by cultural association, solicited an impression of respect, even awe, for brain science. In segments, the music's aesthetic qualities expanded into moving, beautiful self-contained melodic compositions, while other segments were strange, inviting admiration for the sound. Further segments presented machine noise that suggested recognizable settings. Music suggested context and location and emphasized, punctuated and stirred as it engaged the body-brain and contributed to an aesthetic mood that drew the spectator into the performance.

In elaborating on the emotional functions of music and definitions, Robinson explains how Peter Kivy argues that music cannot arouse specific sadness or joy in the listener even when it expresses generic qualities of such emotions, because it is not a provocation for an emotion feeling. There needs to be a further stimulus – that is, a 'plausible intentional object for the emotions aroused by music' (Robinson 2012: 655). Leonard Meyer argues to the contrary that the structure of the music itself is understood through emotions such as surprise and bewilderment. Patrik Juslin points out that music communicates with acoustic patterns that implicate automatic brain systems; a sound comparable to a baby's cry or a cry of despair may have a physiological effect (Robinson 2012: 657).

The technical qualities of the music melody and harmony have an impact, as do key changes and its softness and loudness.

Hence this debate about how music works is about the physiological reaction to the music itself versus cultural associations accumulated over time. It reflects the wider issue about ways to reconcile emotional feelings as either physiological or cultural, and since the division between the (six–eight) basic biological responses and more complicated socially induced emotions became contested. Music, too, is a cultural language. Therefore Robinson draws on Noel Carroll's contention that music induces mood because it does not provide a direct cause for an emotion or an emotional feeling. Whether mood connects with the physiology of the body or not, a mood can be supported by music and becomes recognizable. The mood qualities of music in performance can be attributed to both its formal properties and/or cultural exposure.

Crucially, Robinson herself presents a clear argument that music can arouse emotional feelings and mood simultaneously (2012: 674). As well, she suggests that stimulation of emotional feelings and the appreciation of the music aesthetics can happen together. This possibility is evident with theatrical performance, as various sensory and emotional elements combine together. The music might function in dual ways, both supplanting short-lived emotion and inducing a comparatively more prolonged mood effect – a sequence of specific emotions are accommodated within an overarching mood. For example, a verbal expression of fear by a character fits within a mood of hostility, one often greatly enhanced by sound. The sound and music can precondition felt responses or, alternatively, undercut an aesthetic effect.

It can be challenging to describe the difference between the experience of an emotional feeling and a mood. Spatial metaphors can assist; bodily feelings arise and spread, whereas the aesthetic mood might be considered to descend and surround. Music can induce feelings such as ebullience or peacefulness or irritation and these generate measurable but variable brain activity. Assuming that listening to music, which has brain effects, can also activate mood, it follows that music and mood might influence the sensory body's perception. These are moods rather than emotional feelings because the listener is not feeling sad about the music (Robinson 2012: 667). There is no direct provocation. A listener allows the mood of the music to prevail, so he or she (they) is taken over by it.

The science on the brain is revealing and intriguing but often inconclusive. Rimini Protokoll's *Brain Projects*, available online, depicted the brain as a puzzle and emblematic of the scientific search for consciousness. *Brain Projects* presented two scientists alongside a person caught up in police brutality in Rimini Protokoll's innovative form of staging experts rather than trained performers (Dreysse and Malzcher 2008; Mumford 2013: 153). Directed by Helgard Kim Haug and Daniel Wetzel and performed by philosopher musician, Lobna Allamii, and scientists, Felix Hasler and Irini Skaliora, *Brain Projects* presented scientific fascination with the brain in conjunction with a narrative about its vulnerability. In the live show each expert was filmed and projected into a miniature set as it was constructed in captivating action. While there was affect from this viewing, and feeling described within each personal testimony rather than acted, it was the sound that shaped impressions of mood in a sequence of scenes. Allamii's story of violent attack revealed the consequences of a brain injury; in this instance, the skull was fractured during a political street protest. A brain injury became symbolic of the state's violent repression and metaphoric of a society's impaired capacity. The brain was both a concept and an object handled on stage and given to the audience. After years of psychiatric research on neural connections and exceptional states of mind and drugs, Hasler now considered efforts to explain the neurochemical capacity to be self-reductionist and generating a neuro-mythology. In disagreement, Skaliora compared the brain to a conductor of an orchestra as it created a system of interpretation and prediction – something like a theatre director. The performance pointed out that the feeling and sensing personal self is far more than the sum of all the nodes and intersecting neural connections in the material composition of the brain. A dispersed intelligence surrounds the individual with its collective capacity – that is, a brain is activated by and within social connections. This might also involve collective emotions and social moods.

Mood also offers a way of describing emotional orientation. The qualities of 'awe, wonder, quietude, surprise and bliss' that are described as arising in response to music also assist a spectator to hear it more acutely (Robinson 2012: 676). Even with an argument as to whether, with the exception of bliss, these qualities might be affective sensation rather than emotional feeling, they arise through sensory engagement within an aesthetic experience. Hence a sequence of affect and emotional feelings accumulates in a felt space of mood. Music is an important part of performance, a key element, but it is only part of the overall theatrical mood. What is significant is that it contributes directly to the aesthetic mood and how it expands the social meaning of performance. Music supports artistic practice reflecting a pervasive mood effect in society.

Economic mood dis/orders: *Alladeen* to *Dear Evan Hansen*

What types of aesthetic mood are reflected by twenty-first-century performance that critiques society? European theatre is described as becoming more melancholic in a twenty-first-century time of doubt about realizing democratic ideals when faced with forces of resistance and highly questionable political and economic practices (Schramm and Michieli 2009). This suggests continuity with melancholy within modernism

(Flatley 2008), so that a twenty-first-century resurgence of melancholic impressions becomes indicative of fluctuations in social mood over time.

Alladeen (1997–2007) was an Obie Award-winning live performance about workers who perform in twenty-first-century global corporate workplaces, and it presented contrasting aesthetic moods of melancholy in a city and hilarity in a call centre. The narrative was about workers in telecommunications call centres in Bangalore, India, that have been transferred from North America, and the ensuing mismatches between cultural identity and linguistic dexterity. A joint project of New York's The Builders Association and London's motiroti, *Alladeen* was directed by Marianne Weems and designed by Keith Khan and Ali Zaidi, and it combined live performance, filmed documentary footage and computer-generated multimedia effects. In referring to the story of Aladdin and the magic of a wish-fulfilling genie transplanted into telecommunications, *Alladeen* suggested Edward Said's analysis of the way Western culture imagines and objectifies the East through orientalism. At the same time *Alladeen*'s significance reflected the politics of the twenty-first century as it highlighted the impasse when global capitalism and its technologies bring diverse worlds closer together but continue to reinforce racial and cultural hegemonies.

A call centre was created by actors with headphones sitting on the stage at computer terminals. An Indian female worker, struggling to become sufficiently American in her English-language intonation and emotional tone, was at risk of being fired, while the central character, Joey, tried to entice her to leave with him; he moved from a shared life in India to solitude in London. *Alladeen*'s sophisticated linguists switched effortlessly between languages as they walked the unwelcoming streets of New York or London (or any major city) so their economic success was framed by personal and social moods of loneliness. Back in the call-centre scenarios, the disembodied voices of North Americans became the source of wry humour, with quirky requests and revelations of weird behaviour. Drug-taking Americans tried to book airline tickets or called in panic for road directions. The production's aesthetic effects located the moods of workers and callers within their economic circumstances.

A major element of *Alladeen* was its documentary footage of interviews with actual call-centre workers, a group of educated, articulate young Indians with the cleverness to assume an American accent and persona at will. Some demonstrated skills that rival those of an accomplished theatre actor and, clearly, actors and theatre artists are also workers in a global economy. English is widely spoken in India – a legacy of colonialism and this prevalence makes India attractive to corporate enterprises from English-speaking countries wishing to pay lower wages in cheap-skate global economics. At the same time India remains an autonomous social and artistic culture without the kind of whole-scale saturation of American television and cinema experienced in, for example, Australia or Canada. There was considerable humour in *Alladeen* from teaching Indian workers about American popular culture and lifestyle which was foreign to them with, for example, the emotional relationships in the sitcom *Friends*, and the rules for baseball.

The documentary presented close-ups of the heads and shoulders of real workers on a stage-length rectangular screen that towered above the live actors in affective distortion. If these offered an intimate view of the workers and made the live actors seem more remote, their facial expressions less visible, nonetheless, the live action and offstage voices had an emotional impact. In this performance about global economies, the currency was the liveness of person-to-person phone transactions. While the documentary footage detailed the worker's lives, the live performance revealed how the emotional exchanges were an inherent part of the work and that workers had to learn another emotional expression in order to pretend to be American.

With emotional subtlety, *Alladeen* offered a superb example of the economic production of selective emotions within global service industries. Workers delivered cheerfulness, politeness and the requisite charm through brightly engaging small talk, part of the sales tactics. Emotional engagement was clearly culturally specific in that the Indian call-centre workers were learning the emotional transactions of another culture. Voice intonations had to be learnt to convey emotional meaning. *Friends* contained an emotional typography that Indian workers needed to acquire for communication; they must leave a phone customer feeling good about him or herself at the end of the 'show'.

Alladeen was indicative of political theatre that juxtaposes social and cultural contradictions rather than delivers a message so that its mood effects convey its meaning. The production presented an insidious twenty-first-century economic imperialism that was colonizing desires and moods. A female worker revealed quiet desperation, explaining her willingness to do call-centre work came from her absorption of 'the American dream' in which 'anyone-can-make-good', a dream that had expanded during Silicon Valley's absorption of computer-industry workers from India. This doubled back on technology's promise of immediate gratification through instant communication, in sharp contrast to the immobility of most workers. *Alladeen* finished with migrant male and female characters singing or dancing in a karaoke bar miming Western popular culture and talking on their mobile phones in disembodied emotional exchange. A melancholic mood of stasis replaced the energetic effort to digitally connect and its optimism.

William James proposes that a '"strenuous mood"' drives thought, and mood orientates the individual self to 'energetic striving' in modernity (Shusterman 2012: 433). An excited mood facilitates reaching out into a bright-looking world and a depressed one inhibits effort as the world seems flat and unwelcoming. A depressed mood slows cognitive processes and a happy mood expands them, but psychological mood that is separated from a social and political context masks these influences on individual disposition.

A mood disorder such as depression or anxiety would seem to be an unlikely topic for serious treatment in a Broadway musical, even with the major precedent set by Stephen Sondheim's music theatre and its darker confronting emotions. Certainly mental health and its institutional treatment are longstanding themes in serious dramatic theatre about personal suffering (Harpin and Foster 2014: 5). Yet depression and other mood disorders were central to a recent award-winning music theatre production, *Dear Evan Hansen*, written by Steven Levenson, which presented twenty-first-century dilemmas and reflected the increasing prevalence of depression. (I viewed it on 27 September 2017 in New York, with Michael Lee Brown as Evan.) Although the production intermittently encompassed strong emotions of depression, grief and loss, the overarching mood was strenuous, 'energetic striving'. In a narrative about emotional difficulties and economic problems in family life, young characters sought a sense of belonging to ward off feelings of isolation, loneliness and emotional struggle as a suicide happened in their midst. The core issue was an age-old one about the human need for friendship. As Aristotle writes: 'For friendship is a virtue, or involves virtue; and also it is one of the most indispensable requirements of life' (1996: 205). *Dear Evan Hansen* confirmed that friendship is believed to be necessary, as it presented a pretend friendship and implied that close friendship was at risk in our technological world. What was also noticeably twenty-first century in this production was the changeable performative self of the central character.

At the insistence of his hard-working single mother, Heidi (Rachel Bay Jones), seventeen-year-old Evan Hansen, perceived as a loner, visited a therapist who encouraged him to write a letter to himself as part of his therapy for depression. One of these letters was snatched by Connor Murphy (Mike Faist), someone even more depressed and marginalized than Evan. Sadly, Connor committed suicide – this was conveyed rather briefly. Evan's letter was found and assumed to have been written by Connor to Evan, his only friend. Evan did not correct this mistaken assumption of friendship because he was attracted to Connor's sister, Zoe (Laura Dreyfuss), who returned Evan's interest. In their grief, the Murphy family welcomed Evan as someone who knew Connor well. Nor did Evan correct this misconception with his peers as they organized a fund-raising project in memory of Connor. As the project gained momentum online and galvanized a large following, Evan had to build on his pretence of friendship. Meanwhile Evan's emotional experience completely changed as he became the popular centre of attention through the Connor Project, which emotionally enhanced the lives of all those involved by creating a collaborative connection that alleviated feelings of isolation. As well as an upbeat effect, the music and the lyrics by Benj Pasek and Justin Paul conveyed pathos, and *Dear Evan Hansen* used the traditional theatrical devices of the letter and Evan talking to the ghost of Connor alongside twenty-first-century screen projections of internet sites and social media. The households of the two families were indicated by a bed or a sofa in relatively sparse staging in front of the changing back wall of the digital set design. As the flawed reality of Evan's pretend emotional world inevitably unravelled, he seemed wiser if not especially regretful over this deception. As Evan remade himself, an unstable emotional identity emerged from the performance of a social self.

Emotions of sadness and regret were deployed into the project of remembrance, which forged community and emotional connections amongst its creators so that the online project fostered a positive mood. The tragic situation of *Dear Evan Hansen* emphasized that it is hard to know someone even in the intimacy of family life – that is, to know his or her (their) psychological mood. The production suggested that this distance has been accentuated in the twenty-first century for all its technological interconnectedness.

Dear Evan Hansen also presented economic inequality as a problem by juxtaposing the economic struggle of Heidi to maintain her household, with the economically well-off, intact Murphy family; Heidi's pride would not let the others assist them. Evan's problems were economic as well as emotional.

The reversal of Evan's emotional life in the narrative still left the economic inequity unresolved, aside from a vague promise that individual striving for an education would improve the lives of both Heidi and Evan in the future. Evan's mood disorder was strongly connected with economic inequity.

As Michel Foucault explains, the Aristotelian concept of economics depends on emotional relationships. He points out that Aristotle understood economics should be about people rather than material goods and concerned with 'leadership, oversight, and control' within social systems that are founded on the core relationships of the domestic household (Foucault 1990: 175). This traditional idea of economics denotes systems of production contingent on land ownership or at least its occupation, enabling food production and the biological production of humans and animals and for trade. In an Aristotelian framework, production is tempered by moderation, moral behaviour and possibly the law, as economic value is attributed to the organization of human labour as much as to its ownership of nonhuman animals and property. The idea of an economic unit based on familial emotions such as love and loyalty, and encompassing sexual relations, means emotions are clearly foundational to economic practices. The *Dear Evan Hansen* production implied that love and loyalty even in an imperiled family unit remain vital to economic survival in the twenty-first century.

Raymond Williams points out that during the twentieth century, economic production came to mean far more than the production of material objects and structural economies and refers to any 'perceived system of production, distribution and exchange', inclusive of the production of culture and its reception (Williams 1977: 11). He describes 'structures of feeling' in his analysis of how economic and cultural production also involves less tangible frameworks and that artistic creation can point to new directions in feeling arising outside the existing structures (1977: 128–35). This concept of social feeling can be aligned with mood. As artistic works make qualities such as affect, emotional feeling and mood central to depictions of social organization and processes of material exchange, these constitute an intangible shadow economic and political realm. Lepecki and Banes contend that it is difficult to consider even the senses in the consumption of performance without considering 'subjacent economies and politics of appearing' and to confront the imbalance between 'the perceptible and the imperceptible' (Lepecki and Banes 2007: 2). Political significance arises from sensory aesthetics in art and in life (Rancière 2014).

Economic production in the twenty-first century is increasingly reliant on digital industries that reduce direct human contact. The plays of Caryl Churchill depict the political consequences of inequitable economic relations over decades (Kritzer 1991; Luckhurst 2015) and point to a resulting cumulative emotional distortion in society. Churchill's (2012) play *Love and Information* depicts scenarios of work along with numerous types of love including sexual love for an avatar composed of digital information. There is a short segment called 'Fired' about a worker who is fired by email and goes to the office of his or her manager, angrily demanding to be told in person:

> You shouldn't fire people by email.
> You can't come bursting in here and shouting.
> I'm just saying it needs to be face to face. (Churchill 2012: 19)

This sequence presents an emotionally distressing situation for the worker powerlessly caught up in an economic strategy of restructuring and redundancy, and casualization, and the manager's strategy to avoid being 'looked in the eye' by the angry worker (Churchill 2012: 19). Electronic modes allow people to avoid live face-to-face communication and its emotional confrontation. The loss of dignity from the dismissal is reinforced through its remote digital delivery. Such communication may be legal but the worker questions whether it is moral to dismiss someone by email or other electronic transmission.

'Fired' implicates a neoliberal regime in which workers are presumed to be expendable. In her succinct summary of major critiques of neoliberal economics which she relates to performance, Lara Nielsen (2012) outlines twenty-first-century ideological fractures that threaten social stability through the changing global patterns of organized labour and virtual capital and which magnify the disadvantage of some social groups. Against a backdrop of mobility for economic benefit, there is an elevation of hate politics against outsiders, and what Pankaj Mishra describes as 'the sense of being humiliated by arrogant and deceptive elites' that spans national and religious divisions for social groups who are not benefitting economically (2017: 11). Mishra argues that economics and socio-political disorder have become more apparent as traditional forms of governing are being undermined and the twentieth-century modernist promise of equality for all fades.

What becomes anomalous in the twenty-first century is how pessimism emerges in the developed world, and notwithstanding the economic and social impact of the coronavirus pandemic COVID-19. At an individual level this might be due to the insecurity of work or social allegiances. At a cultural level, this can be attributed to the realization that the fundamental economic premise of growth is contingent on material resources that are finite and growth continues despite longstanding arguments for a 'steady state' economy. As Amitav Ghosh (2016) explains what he calls the 'great derangement' of global economic thinking about the earth's resources and its founding racist mythologies, he describes feelings of dread. Gosh explains that 'the patterns of life that modernity engenders can only be practiced by a small minority of the world's population' (2016: 92). The connection between economic belief and sensitivity to a fearful mood is made explicit.

Mishra (2017) discerns an 'age of anger' in the twenty-first century. While this raises the ongoing issue of the meaning of anger in relation to other emotions such as hopelessness or anxiety, taken as converging with each other, anger offers a vivid way of describing a social mood effect. As Churchill demonstrates, there is an established trope of character anger about political and economic circumstances in drama. Mishra is arguing that there is a strong sense of polarized values in most national states in the first decades of the twenty-first century and through which, Mishra argues, angry reactions accumulate and compound. Thus it is possible to discern a cultural mood of animosity emerging from fragmented or polarized economic circumstances. While Mishra finds historical modernist precedents in demagoguery and totalitarianism to explain the political present, he does not argue that history is being repeated. Instead Mishra notes how new technologies increasingly facilitate and heighten the possibility of what Friedrich Nietzsche extracts from philosophical history as the public outbursts of 'men of *ressentiment*', and Hannah Arendt terms 'negative solidarity' (2017: 9, 13, italics in original). There is disenchantment within liberal democracy because sufficient numbers of people feel thwarted in what Arendt foresees as '"an unbearable burden," provoking "political apathy, isolationist nationalism, or desperate rebellion"' (Mishra 2017: 334).

In his response to the rhetoric of a twenty-first-century age of terror and 'megalomaniacal violence' and hatred, Rustom Bharucha opts not to trace dramaturgical themes of terror in theatre and the avant garde, but to investigate performed moments that are 'unscripted' and 'undetermined' (2014: 14, 19). In a performance studies approach, Bharucha acknowledges Western theory about the underlying violence of the democratic state and Judith Butler on performativity, as he seeks illustrative social events and 'social interactions, behaviours, strategies, deceptions, manipulations' in everyday life and from the Philippines, South Africa and India (2014: 19). In the slippage between theatrical performance and socio-political events, performance takes place in perceptual spaces that are emotionally inflected and moody.

The aesthetic mood that conveys a social mood of, for example, anger in relation to the economic system can make audience members uncomfortable. It can be challenging to present what seems like the impasse of entrenched political and economic problems and points of view. But conveying a mood of disquiet or disappointment or outrage through performance can communicate people's experiences of the wider socio-economic culture. It can help to clarify that a seemingly subjective feeling is experienced by others. Alternatively, a production might immerse audiences in a comic mood while continuing to critique political events – it might parody events. The concept of mood, and as motivation for action, captures a spectrum of artistic responses to social experience. Counteracting a pessimistic mood that reinforces a sense of inaction and defeat seems like a task for political theatre.

Immoral objects and The Wooster Group

Twenty-first-century performance often breaks up the seamless synthesis of aesthetic elements including modes of emotional delivery and mood immersion in theatre. Contemporary performance is not necessarily concerned with providing the audience with a satisfying mood experience. It can seem contemptuous of audiences (Freshwater 2009). The Wooster Group's Obie Award-winning *To You, the Birdie! (Phèdre)*, directed by Elizabeth LeCompte, was first staged in 2001, and it presented badminton played live onstage and emotional exchanges enacted like a sports game with its energetic striving. The title refers to a conventional pre-game exchange in which one player informs the other player that the game has begun before hitting the shuttlecock or birdie across the net. On a screen above the stage, the goddess Venus (Suzzy Roche) refereed the badminton games, calling out instructions such as 'fault' and 'player to court', and naming emotions in the same tone as if they were instructions in a game and to be hit backwards and forwards between the players. In *To You, the Birdie!*, the words for emotions were part of the physical action but detached from embodied expression. Emotions were interchangeable with visible objects.

The moral ambiguity of *To You, the Birdie!* evoked a mood of unease as it pointed to the earlier Greco-Roman versions of Phèdre's story with hints of classical sculpture. It was an adaptation of Paul Schmidt's version of an eighteenth-century classic, Racine's *Phèdre* (1993), and included Phèdre's nursemaid, Oenone (Frances McDormand or Sheena See). In the basic narrative, Phèdre falls in love with her stepson, Hippolytos (also spelt Hippolytus), while her husband, King Theseus, is away at war, and on his return Phèdre, sick with love, accuses the innocent Hippolytos of the violating affection, proclaiming her own innocence, and he is banished. This drama about a woman at the mercy of her own passion and lying, is far less produced than plays about moral courage, bravery and the fulfilment of duty, such as Sophocles's *Antigone* with countless interpretations (Steiner 1984). As moral values, self-sacrifice and courage are judged of a far higher order than scandalous infidelity and dishonesty. In addition, Phèdre's desire intersects with the persona of the monstrous stepmother and with sexual abuse as she unravels the social order through her shameless behaviour (Woodworth 2010). Goldie explains, it is a 'natural idea that the object of an emotion is that onto which one's thoughts and feelings are typically directed', and this can be directed to a nonhuman entity (2000: 17). The object of Phèdre's obsessive thoughts, of her love and lust, was Hippolytos so that she created unnatural disorder; Phèdre's immorality is explicit in some versions when she accuses Hippolytos of rape.

Impressions of mood in The Wooster Group's *To You, the Birdie!* started with upbeat, energetic striving, then progressed towards a moribund stasis and ended in bleakness and all the while offering a slyly amusing undercurrent. The vocal and physical actions were separated, as performer, Scott Shepherd, voiced the words and thoughts of Phèdre (Kate Valk) in falsetto into a microphone as well as those of Theseus (Roy Faudree or Willem Dafoe) in base tones. The feeling and words were further separated as Shepherd delivered the spoken text of these characters in The Wooster Group's trademark deadpan tone. A near-naked, athletic Hippolytos (Ari Fliakos) delivered his own lines into a microphone in gentle cadence, which reinforced his vulnerability and also his possession of the story. Hippolytos held the moral ground in *Hippolytos* by Euripides as its beautiful, chaste and unsuspecting character (1997a, 1997b). Although Euripides may have had to revise an earlier bleaker version, the extant play – considered one of his greatest works – has the lovesick Phèdre overhearing Hippolytus condemning her and women, and her love dissipates and her strong emotional feeling turns vindictive. She says, 'Why should he ruin my life and laugh? He'll suffer what now I'm suffering' (Euripides 1997b: 30, lines 729–30). Phèdre kills herself but leaves an accusatory letter so that Theseus believes her and banishes his son, and the latter part of the play concerns his remorse and reconciliation with the dying Hippolytus, injured after an accident. What is notable about such Greek drama is the way the gods determine human fate, personify human emotions, and become emotionally offended and betrayed, and thus religious belief offsets human responsibility.

In lieu of emotive delivery, *To You, the Birdie!* included stylized movement and balletic action that contrasted with the servants handling the bodies of the king and the queen as if helping incapacitated patients, tending to their bodily functions and incontinence with medical instruments (Cody 2003). Phèdre's despair was evident in her restricted physical movement and hysterical shaking, and both Phèdre and Theseus seemed puppet-like. This production had the common features of a Wooster Group production directed by LeCompte, with its humour, clever mix of live performance, and recorded and remediated live audio and visual projection, and monotonal unemotional delivery spoken into microphones.

Emotionless voices point to interactions with machines in the contemporary world. Jennifer Parker-Starbuck confirms that 'the Group suggests a mediatized form of objectification that is often obscured' as it overturns how identity is polarized, using the 'live/mediatized divides that fix bodies as object' (2011: 106). The performer's body filmed live became an object image on the stage. In the separation of voice and body, Phèdre's staccato movement suggested a mechanical entity, a cyborg. Ric Knowles outlines how the expanded meanings of The Wooster Group productions critique 'mediatization and brutalization of contemporary urban life' through the reinterpretation of classic plays (2004: 148). The Wooster Group emerged out of American avant-garde practice and often draws on its tradition of writing (Savran 1986; Parker-Starbuck 2011: 102–26), and productions invite diverse responses from spectators (Knowles 2004: 149). At the same time, The Wooster Group specifies that their work comes out of New York's lower Manhattan, so its complex irony is effective with audiences who have some knowledge of theatrical performance.

The disdainful action surrounding Phèdre compounded an impression of grotesqueness. One critic criticized the production as being full of gimmicks, and another points out that exposed body parts and an enactment of bodily functions may shock some spectators (Sommer 2002). More expressly, however, *To You, the Birdie!* explored failure: in the game thwarted by Venus, in Phèdre's failure to fulfil her imagined union with Hippolytus, in the failed state rule of Theseus, and in the complicated sexual politics of revenge and punishment. Sara Jane Bailes (2011) explains that contemporary performance explores ideas of failure by diverting or disrupting the elements that are expected of theatrical performance. As it exposed a personal politics of failed emotions in Phèdre's self-serving manipulation of events, The Wooster Group's refusal to perform emotional feelings created a deliberate theatrical failure by unravelling how these seamlessly bind together words and bodies in theatre.

Theatrical performance engages with the way that emotional feeling might be reproduced or masked, or in the example of

The Wooster Group, objectified as surface phenomena. The game motif demonstrated the function of rules for emotional exchange in society as it aligned theatre with sport in the arousal of strong feelings. In addition, the historical references collapsed together passion for someone and for performance, and a further interpretation became apparent with the layered theatre histories and fragments of earlier texts that were visually and aurally referenced. *To You, the Birdie!* suggested that the emotional feeling of historical and/or fictional figures remained inaccessible; emotional feeling had been lost.

To You, the Birdie! did not offer condemnation of transgressive sexual and emotional love. The proposition that emotionally felt responses in performance assist in understanding those in life becomes questionable (Matravers 2012), and in the context of a larger question as to whether theatrical performance has a moral purpose to instruct its audiences and to even align its emotion with that of life. In considering the difficulties of emotional responses to extreme body-based live arts in the United States, Jennifer Doyle finds it invites affect as it repulses and emotionally 'moves' at the same time (Doyle 2013: xi). Bodies lie together, bleed, abort and are infused in the works that Doyle analyses and finds create closeness. In an opposing view, Matthew Kieran considers that in the asymmetry of emotions between life and artistic representation, it is through distancing that moral values can be emotionally apprehended, and he offers the example of challenging racist values (2012: 685). He is concerned that in the aestheticization of violence, a contrary response can be evoked – for example, thrill or amusement. The way performance evokes sympathy for a character may potentially be separated from the consequences of bad behaviour. Kieran is concerned that antisocial identities in cultural representation will be morally corrosive – a concern expressed by Plato. But it can be argued to the contrary that this makes artistic interpellation of extreme experience even more crucial within a social context.

To You, the Birdie! sidelined emotional evocation with its dissembled theatrical elements. Emotional experience, then, was devolved to the audience and the performance might have been enjoyable or frustrating or distasteful or even titillating or none of these; the production invited awareness of emotional responses that were independent of the performance. In summary, the production was antithetical to immersion in an emotional artistic mood. It relinquished responsibility for audience emotions. Meanwhile the narrative drew audience attention to the destructive power of emotion.

Post-Brechtian contemporary performance often sets up modes of distancing and, in combination with technological intervention, induces affect, as it leaves other types of engagement, including emotional feeling and mood, open-ended. Doubtless, *To You, the Birdie!* elicited visceral affects in reactions which potentially ranged from looking away momentarily to squeamish aversion. Such affective responses circulating amidst the audience might unsettle and disturb. Affect, however, may not be easy to recall afterwards, whereas emotional mood can persist in memory.

In another version of the Phèdre story, Sarah Kane's (2002) *Phaedra's Love* updates the narrative, and it ends in a frenetic mood of savagery and sexual fantasy. As with her other work, it expands on the dimensions of emotional trauma and points to the psychosis of characters as emblematic of social disturbance (Waters 2006; Marshall 2011; Duggan 2012). Kane increases the violence and not only does Phaedra kill herself, but her daughter Strophe is raped and killed, Hippolytus is castrated and Theseus kills himself. Kane's version of the story makes the links between sex and violence explicit. It also uses dark humour in theatrical excess and in the exchanges between Phaedra and the indifferent – possibly depressed – narcissistic Hippolytus, who is sexually complicit in numerous sex acts and masturbates in front of the television. Christine Woodworth writes that the junk food addicted, video-game-playing 'Hippolytus appears incapable of emotion' (2010: 142). Kane's *Phaedra's Love* presents a world in which emotions arise illogically and oppress, and lead to either self-harm or attacks on others. Kane's play, however, points to a larger consumer world in which a continuous barrage of media images and reports of rape, violence and war invade the psyche and have a deadening effect on mood. It grapples with the personal consequences of confronting, distressing and traumatic experiences in life by putting theatrical extremes that shock centre stage.

Theatre performance diverges from screen culture at a time when the choice of emotional mood experience proliferates. Films, television and screen media allow viewers to engage with the emotions of characters on demand; for example, they can binge-watch television series, immersing themselves in imaginary emotional worlds. Therefore the evaporating emotional feeling and mood in *To You, the Birdie!* seem important. Live performance does not set out to compete with the emotionality of the screen and remains far less voracious and more puzzling, as it facilitates spectator deliberation and mood that requires consideration after the event.

Share economies and Marina Abramovic

As a social gathering ranging from the large-scale to the small-scale event, theatrical performance impacts on an individual and group mood. This is similar to how the exuberance and adulation of a crowd at a sports match or attending a concert appear to be a shared mood – that of despair if the team loses. The emotional mood of such events seems infectious. Carolyn Price describes a mass outpouring of grief when a large number of people become upset at the death of a celebrity; she notes that some are suspected of wanting to be associated with a celebrity, so there is a component of inauthentic sorrow (2015: 157). This raises a question as to whether exuberance or grief comes from joining the social gathering, and points to the way emotional feeling and mood are still deemed either direct and first-hand (primary) or indirect and second-hand (secondary). The feeling effects of watching live and screen performance would seem to be second-hand with less at stake compared with first-hand experience. But as sports spectatorship reveals, feelings and moods are intensely directly felt.

Live performance that removes some of the distinctions between performer and spectator blurs notions of direct and indirect emotional engagement, even in larger productions with audience members selected to participate on the stage. The common practice of singling out someone in a venue with a thousand or more spectators and putting him or her (them) on the stage to humorous effect contributes to the emotional risks of attending live performance. Participants overcome their initial uncertainty, even embarrassment – some refuse. There is a general admiration for the person selected and relief at not being chosen.

In the twenty-first century, small-scale interactive performance events directly involve spectators in the physical action. It can alter the implicit theatrical contract between spectator and performer so that participants are expected to share the creative process. It seems comparable to the ethos behind the idea of a share economy in early twenty-first-century economic practices – for example, the devolved provision of travel accommodation through 'Airbnb'. Participants in the share economy of small-scale performance are also responsible for how it unfolds and it becomes like first-hand experience. Such involvement can happen through online participation as well as attendance at a live event.

Small-scale live performance refines the inherently theatrical idea of a shared economy of the senses as it creates an intimate mood. Affect and emotional feeling arise from attending as there can be the emotional tension in not quite knowing what to do or what to expect. A participant might feel nervous that no one is in control. Interactive performance can immerse spectators in situations that can be both thrilling and excruciating.

In a participatory performance that evoked intense reactions and stirred media controversy in 2010, the esteemed performance artist, Marina Abramovic, created *The Artist Is Present*, at the Museum of Modern Art in New York. She sat silently in a chair without moving, facing another chair and, one at a time, viewers were invited to sit opposite in silence and look directly at her. The event took place each day over six weeks, and Abramovic's endurance feat of sitting was shared with an audience in the surrounding gallery space, some viewers staying for hours. In a documentary about her work which includes segments about younger performers restaging her earlier performances, Abramovic says 'you're looking at many Marinas' and that the sitting in *The Artist Is Present* creates an 'altered state of mind', to which viewers respond (*Marina Abramovic: The Artist Is Present* 2012). In the one-to-one engagement, some sat looking in this intimate way for a matter of minutes and some for much longer, and the documentary captured how this was often an emotionally overwhelming experience. Whether performances such as Abramovic's *The Artist Is Present* with its minimal action and facial expression facilitated self-reflection or more fundamental brain and body physiological reactions (Di Benedetto 2010), a process of sitting and looking evoked affect, and emotional feelings for some viewers.

Abramovic's body-based oeuvre involves extreme action and she performed naked in early works (Phelan 2001: 44; Celant 2001; Di Benedetto 2010: 76–7). A postcolonial performance in 2015 by Robyne Latham in Australia, *The Aborigine Is Present* that was part homage and part contestation had an equally strong impact – Abramovic had expressed regret for ill-informed racist comments made in the 1970s (Stevens 2018).

This type of body-based performance originated in the 1960s and 1970s, and included Yoko Ono's *Cut Piece* in which she asked spectators to cut her clothing with scissors, and which she revived in 2012. Other similar works included Stelarc in body suspensions, hanging mid-air in public space from hooks in his flesh (see Section Two). In analysing her experience of Kira O'Reilly's performances, *My Mother* in 2003 and the series *Untitled Action* in 2005, Rachel Zerihan (2010) finds that these function like emotional rituals. *My Mother* invited a spectator to talk about his or her mother before the artist asked approval to cut her own skin. *Untitled Action* invited a spectator to make a small cut in the skin of the artist as it evoked spectator responsibility for the wounding. Patrick Duggan describes his phenomenological experience and visceral reactions to what happened (2012: 141–7). Zerihan found herself fearful of causing pain in *Untitled Action* and reinterprets the classical sequence of catharsis in her personal experience of the build-up of ambivalent intensity to witnessing the wounding of the artist's body. Zerihan is clear that not all spectators react in the same way, and her explanation acknowledges the difficulty of encompassing the physiological, emotional and psychological responses that arise simultaneously in the immediate moment when writing about live performance at a later time.

This small-scale performance creates a mood of intimacy as it seeks to induce reactions that are unguarded and spontaneous (first-hand), like those in life. But what constitutes first-hand reactions in performance given that observing others activates mirror-neurons and emotional centres of the brain? Even this intimate performance has a calculated effect. Price summarizes emotional theory that deems someone who presents a smiling demeanour when he or she is feeling sad as inauthentic or fake but explains that the '*provenance*' of such responses frames them in life (Price 2015: 161, italics in original). Therefore the context of a performance or event as much as agreed values make emotional responses less calculated. Reactions within intimate performances can be considered authentic even with the acknowledgement that the spontaneity is being deliberately facilitated.

Zerihan considers that the experience at a computer screen does not have the intimate closeness of small-scale live performance whereas others disagree and describe intense embodied responses to screen performance (Chatzichristodoulou and Zerihan 2012: 2). This point of divergence between live and screen intimacy is not so much resolved as highlighted in Maria Chatzichristodoulou and Zerihan's (2012) analysis, as they draw on Slavoj Zizek's fear of a totalitarian domination through the internet, and Julia Kristeva's idea of intimacy as an awareness of subjective experience and thinking. Chatzichristodoulou and Zerihan conclude: 'At this time of political contention, financial unrest and social anxiety', the intimacy achieved through such performance overcomes the separation of 'I' from the other (2012: 11). Intimate performance promises an intense encounter with a stranger, and a precarious mood. Small-scale performances that magnify the unpredictable quality of emotional exchanges between a performer and a spectator as co-creator, mimic the uncertainty of exchanges in life.

Collaborative eco-moods

Small-scale performance in the twenty-first century additionally encompasses bio-art created with insects or cellular life and directly using or replicating scientific practices in installations and performance, and often with multimedia (Dumitriu 2012). Bio-art includes growing bacterial cultures in a range of site-specific locations and for filming. It grapples with scientific understanding of the human body intermingled with bacterial life and other nonhuman substances as it questions the ethics of industrialized biotechnological production (Senior 2014). Art that presents living organisms is exploring the substratum for life and how the visible boundary of the human body is constantly breached in a type of compulsory sharing. Bio-art demonstrating the evocation of affects ranging from fascination to repulsion follows a trend away from emotional expressiveness in live art.

Theatrical performance about the natural environment, however, continues to point to the fundamental significance of human emotional bonds and relationships within twenty-first-century worlds. It uses the capacity for emotional impact and shared mood to elaborate on the scientifically predicted future. Downing Cless writes of how he 'ecodirects' and he 'coaxed ecological themes to the forefront' even in classic drama, which at first seems human-centred (2012: 159). In this way human relationships and emotional responses are re-contextualized within pressing issues of environmental concern. Cless seeks to challenge what he terms 'ecohubris' as he refers to what Val Plumwood calls '"backgrounding"', when nature is put into the background of human life (Cless 2012: 167). Cless writes that the 'unique power of ecotheater is the way nature is deconstructed, reconstructed, and generated anew – de-alienated, re-enchanted, and activated through performance' (2012: 160). The growing interest in what Theresa J. May terms 'ecodramaturgy' centres on 'ecological reciprocity and community' together with critiques of the economics of resource use and globalization (Arons and May 2012: 4). Reciprocity reflects concern that economic consumption seems to proceed unhindered, even when there is wide agreement that its existing patterns cannot be sustained. An ecological focus can be part of theatre's production resources, its message and the aesthetic mood.

In a shift from love of nature in the early twentieth century to fear about climate change by the twenty-first century, theatrical performance offers a potent way to highlight emotive responses to environmental issues and how fear can immobilize as well as activate and motivate (Tait 2015). It offers a way to link local events to what happens globally politically and within longstanding political and philosophical ecological approaches (Stevens, Tait and Varney 2018). Performance about environmental sustainability can reflect the emotional implications of living with future threats and loss of species habitat.

Shonni Enelow's (2014) performance script *Carla and Lewis* was a key part of the Ecocide project that demonstrated a collaborative way of working to integrate research on environmental issues and climate change science with performance studies scholarship and performance-making. The Ecocide collaboration produced the concept of 'eco-cruelty' from Una Chaudhuri (Chaudhuri 2014: 27). Chaudhuri radically renews Antonin Artaud's vision of shared felt intensity achieved through performance, and combined with an 'enigmatic and provocative' theatre of cruelty which draws on the 'surplus of affect' of a collective event and, in this instance, to imbibe the ideas of eco-theatre and eco-performance and to accord agency to the nonhuman (Chaudhuri 2014: 27). The potential for a hopeful collaborative eco-mood becomes apparent.

Carla and Lewis exposes the unequal economics of climate change in which those with less resources face the greatest impact. Two Berlin performers who are (human) butterflies, Carla and Lewis, appear at the New York apartment of art curator, Elsa Turner, who is preparing an installation about the destruction of homes in low-lying areas of Bangladesh due to climate change. A despairing neighbour scientist predicts the end of the world with DNA mutation, whereas Elsa argues that art must communicate about the need for urgent action. Elsa locates Amina, who was a casualty of climate change, knocked to the ground in her Bangladeshi home due to water inundation from a large spike in tidal seas. Amina explains that she and her family are too poor to leave. Even as it affirms the interconnectedness of the human and the nonhuman, the play warns of a dystopian future unless the necessary action is taken in the present.

The eco-mood of *Carla and Lewis* might be fear-inducing but the Ecocide project is optimistic as a collaborative venture. It models cooperative problem solving in the twenty-first century, through a type of shared economy of artistic practice and ideas – one that supports emotional sustainability and recycled concepts. The redemptive possibility of artistic collaboration and creativity counterbalance how intersecting fiscal, political and sensory economies induce individual moods of despair for the future.

Depictions of the future in popular screen culture are often apocalyptic visions of a destroyed world and survivors living within an unrelenting threatening mood amidst tumultuous upheaval and conflict. Anne Washburn's (2015) play and lyrics for music theatre, *Mr Burns: A Post-Electric Play*, might be set in an apocalyptic future but the mood is boisterous with music by Michael Friedman and includes song and dance, and humorous popular media references (Bay-Cheng 2015; Barrera 2018). Sarah Bay-Cheng describes it as 'virtual realism' and confirms that theatre survives in *Mr Burns* (2015: 689). Act One is set in the aftermath of nuclear disaster when the electricity has failed, and five survivors have retreated to a forest. They mourn lost lives and try to establish a shared cultural background, which turns out to be an episode of *The Simpsons*, the longest running television series, called 'Cape Feare', in which prison escapee Bob tried to kill Bart Simpson who suggests the singing of songs from musicals. The survivors share remembered fragments and lines. In Act Two, seven years later, they have become a theatre troupe rehearsing episodes of *The Simpsons*. By Act Three, seventy years later, the remnants of the old culture and the Simpson's narrative inclusive of power plant operator, Mr Burns, have been forged into a stylized musical, functioning as a type of mythology.

The circumstances of the projected disaster might be tragic but the mood of performance is defiantly adventurous with apocalyptic events in the background, which makes it possible to contemplate what could happen. The amusing premise of *Mr Burns* serves to lessen the fear and hopelessness and open up perspectives on what becomes important in the 'what if' circumstances of technological deprivation. In the immediate aftermath, gathering together in collective endeavour and shared stories remains crucial and forges emotional bonds. While the narrative of *Mr Burns* suggests that making performance creates a future, its metanarrative alludes to how mood can be changed through theatrical performance.

Does it matter that culture's aesthetic legacy in *Mr Burns* is animated media? The suggestion that the classical canon of performance and art has only survived as fragments raises interesting questions about what will be preserved and shared in the future. The future in *Mr Burns* involves the loss of the artistic legacies that capture culture's moods over time.

Anticipation

Twenty-first-century live theatrical performance spans unexpected to familiar action, although knowledge of the story still attracts audiences in an age-old pattern going back to Aristotle. The familiarity of cartoon animation or Shakespeare's classical drama compounds interest. When Dolan describes 'spectatorial anticipation', however, she nominates performance that seeks to change the familiar world and its narratives (2008: 5). Twenty-first-century spectators should anticipate innovative performance that surprises even disorientates in its mood.

A short film, *Stendhal's Vertigo* (2015), directed by Alexis Taillant, investigated a mysterious mood condition in which travellers visiting great works of art in European cities were overcome to the point where they became uneasy and dizzy and some fainted and needed medical treatment even hospital care. The film recreates accounts by sufferers of the syndrome, and medical professionals and psychiatrists. In 1817, the author Stendhal (Marie-Henri Beyle) observed in himself awe and ecstasy, followed by palpitations and vertigo, in encounters with great art, and the syndrome was named after him in 1979. Was this caused by the excitement of realizing a long-held real-time encounter with (celebrity) art? In *Stendhal's Vertigo*, prosaic explanations included the effect of the crowd or the sudden change of place and climate as well as the bodily impact of mass travel. Other explanations reached back to nineteenth-century hysteria and its physical symptoms, including paralysis, and to early-twentieth-century psychoanalytic ideas that the explicit nude art triggers unconscious repressed personal memories of sexuality or trauma. One explanation suggested a spiritual experience. Another explanation suggested that the reaction occurred when viewers had been enticed by a photographic image, but discovered that the size and proportions of the actual artwork were different. Sensory reactions were distorted causing a physical reaction in the body; the affect of viewing induced dizziness. Perhaps it was the surprise of the first-hand experience.

This clever film suggested bodily disorientation in lieu of the expected encounter. There was some prior familiarity and therefore a pre-existing and imagined relationship. The imagining beforehand might have physiological consequences including for the brain, compounding the expectation of what might happen. Was the anticipation of this expected feeling in some way betrayed in the moment of its realization?

The mood effect of performance can be similarly mysterious inducing tears and other physiological reactions. *Stendhal's Vertigo* suggested that individuals seek out heightened experience, the promise of an exalted mood – Stendhal's vertigo might be happiness. Happiness implicates past memory as well as future goals, but awareness of happiness in the present requires someone to think about how he or she (they) feels at that moment, which of course undermines feeling the unfolding feeling. In considering if a happier mood has been achieved, it eludes the grasp. As Ahmed explains, happiness 'can involve a gestural of deferral' and remain anticipated (2010: 33). But Ahmed is also critical of the mythology of delayed happiness within cultural belief and writes: 'Happiness may be preserved as a social promise only through its postponement: so we imagine that the happiness we were promised will eventually come to us'

(2010: 32). She is concerned that such belief dupes people into accepting the economic and social status quo. The anticipation of achieving happiness in the future is what makes it possible to comply, since the longer the wait, the greater the promised happiness. The important quality remains its anticipation.

A mood of anticipation about a forthcoming experience might function as a substitute for happiness but it is a precondition of performance and the other arts. As Susan Feagin writes, 'The key is to understand feelings as a way of apprehending a work: not an effect of it' (2012: 647). She recognizes that heightened feelings can be a bodily response to what James Laird terms an '"eliciting event"', but when these ideas are applied to reading (drama) literature or other art, a cause-and-effect sequence does not really explain the 'cross-temporal' effect (Feagin 2012: 648, 649). A mood of anticipation creates orientation that encourages engagement and connection even when performance does not adhere to conventions and displeases. Anticipation of performance encourages attunement to the emotions, emotional feelings and affect, and it encourages immersion in the aesthetic mood that carries over into lived experience.

A cycle of anticipation in the making and watching of performance compounds its appeal and capacity for a shared aesthetic mood. Affect and/or emotional feeling encourage absorption in the immediacy of the performance, and mood and thought continue in its aftermath. Theatrical performance encourages us to anticipate shared futures.

Conclusion: Intensity

Emotion has explored the ways in which the emotions, emotional feelings, affect and mood can be appreciated as distinctive in the creation and interpretation of theatrical performance and through multi-layered synthesis in its impact. A concentrated effect is integral to a perception of having a powerful experience of performance. Section One, Legacies, explained that theatrical performance communicates what is socially understood about emotions through spoken and other expressive embodied languages. In turn, social understanding becomes enlarged through theatrical composition. Section Two, Affect, explored affect as short-lived bodily sensation and impersonal affect and distinguished it from a personal emotional feeling and empathy in theatrical performance. Section Three, Mood, considered the more lasting aesthetic mood of theatrical performance that evokes individual and social moods and is shared by an audience. As explained, theatrical emotion can be socially shared and provide an opportunity to subjectively imagine the experience of another. Performance repeatedly cultivates such engagement, and recent physically immersive and intimate live art events radically expand this capacity.

While emotion in theatrical performance is artistically created and therefore differs from that in life, it emerges from lived experience and then merges back into it. Performance distils and heightens affect and emotional effects. The elements of performance are artistically crafted to create a diverse range of emotions; from a cathartic cycle in which audiences become involved in the build-up and release of emotional tension to confronting inexpression in live art and its unreliable moods. As indicated, contemporary performance might engage through affect more than emotional feeling, but stripping away social languages of emotions nonetheless compels curiosity as it devolves the responsibility for feeling to the spectator.

In dissembling and reassembling the emotions, emotional feelings, affect and mood in theatrical performance, the function of each separately and together can become apparent. They can be analysed in an oscillating continuum or recognized as occurring more or less simultaneously. In this way the artistic layering of emotion contributes to the intensity of theatrical performance.

REFERENCES

Ahmed, S. (2004), *The Cultural Politics of Emotion*, New York: Routledge.

Ahmed, S. (2010), *The Promise of Happiness*, Durham: Duke University Press.

Ahmed, S. J. (2017), 'Stanislavsky in the Modern Theatre of Bangladesh: A Mapping of Postcolonial Appropriation and Assimilation', in J. Pitches and S. Aquilina (eds), *Stanislavsky in the World*, 417–43, London: Bloomsbury Methuen Drama.

Alladeen (1999–2007), https://www.thebuildersassociation.org/prod_alladeen_artists.html, last accessed 10 May 2020.

Aristophanes (1969), *The Birds*, ed. and trans. W. Arrowsmith in *Three Comedies*, 11–127, Ann Arbor: University of Michigan Press.

Aristotle (1987), 'On the Art of Poetry', in *Classical Literary Criticism*, trans. T. S. Dorsch, 31–75, Harmondsworth: Penguin.

Aristotle (1995), *Poetics*, trans. S. Halliwell, Cambridge, MA: Harvard University Press.

Aristotle (1996), *The Nicomachean Ethics*, trans. H. Rackham, London: Wordsworth Editions.

Arons, W. and T. May (2012), 'Introduction', in W. Arons and T. May (eds), *Readings in Performance and Ecology*, 1–10, New York: Palgrave.

Artaud, A. (1976), *Selected Writings*, trans. H. Weaver, New York: Farrar Straus and Giroux.

Bailes, S. J. (2011), *Performance, Theatre and the Poetics of Failure*, London: Routledge.

Bain, A. (1868), *Mental and Moral Science: A Compendium of Psychology and Ethics*, London: Longmans, Green.

Barbieri, D. (2017), *Costume in Performance: Materiality, Culture and the Body*, London: Bloomsbury.

Barnett, D. with J. Massy-Westropp (1987), *The Art of Gesture: The Practices and Principles of 18th Century Acting*, Heidelberg: Carl Winter Universitatsverlag.

Barrera, C. (2018), '"For We Are American": Postmodern Pastiche and National Identity in Anne Washburn's Mr. Burns, a Post-Electric Play', *Journal Comparative Drama in English* 6 (1): 131–45.

Barrett, L. F. (2018), *How Emotions Are Made*, New York: Mariner Books.

Bartlett, M. (2016), *Wild*, London: Nick Hern Books.

Bay-Cheng, S. (2015), 'Virtual Realisms: Dramatic Forays into the Future', *Theatre Journal* 67 (4): 687–98.

Belfiore, E. (1992), *Tragic Pleasures: Aristotle on Plot and Emotion*, Princeton: Princeton University Press.

Bell, J. M. (2007), 'Melodrama', in G. Cody and E. Sprinchorn (eds), *The Columbia Encyclopedia of Modern Drama*, 889–91, New York: Colombia University Press.

Bennett, J. (2005), *Empathic Vision: Affect, Trauma and Contemporary Art*, Stanford, CA: Stanford University Press.

Bennett, J. (2010), *Vibrant Matter*, Durham: Duke University Press.

Bennett, S. (1990), *Theatre Audiences*, London: Routledge.

Bennett, S. (2019), *Theory for Theatre Studies: Sound*, London: Bloomsbury.

Berlant, L. (2011), *Cruel Optimism*, Durham: Duke University Press.

Bharucha, R. (2014), *Terror and Performance*, London: Routledge, ebook accessed 8 January 2019.

Billington, M. (2014), 'Medea Review', *The Guardian*, 22 July, https://www.theguardian.com/stage/2014/jul/22/medea-carrie-cracknell-helen-mccrory-national-theatre-review, accessed 6 January 2019.

Blackman, L. (2012), *Immaterial Bodies: Affect, Embodiment, Mediation*, London: Sage.

Blair, R. (2009), 'Cognitive Neuroscience and Acting', *TDR: The Drama Review* 53 (4): 93–103.

Blair, R. and A. Cook, eds (2016), *Theatre, Performance and Cognition*, London: Bloomsbury.

Bleeker, M., J. F. Sherman and E. Nedelkopoulou, eds (2015), *Performance and Phenomenology*, London: Routledge.

Boal, A. (2002), *Games for Actors and Non-Actors*, trans. A. Jackson, London: Routledge.

Boal, A. (2008), *Theatre of the Oppressed*, trans. C. A. and M. O. L. McBride and E. Fryer, London: Pluto Press.

Brecht, B. (1986), *The Caucasian Chalk Circle*, ed. and trans. J. and T. Stern with W. H. Auden, London: Bloomsbury Methuen Drama.

Brecht, B. (1987), *Brecht on Theatre*, trans. J. Willett, New York: Hill and Wang.

Brennan, T. (2004), *The Transmission of Affect*, Ithaca: Cornell University Press.

Brown, I. (2010), 'Ambivalence of the Motherhood Experience', in A. O'Reilly (ed.), *Twenty-First-Century Motherhood: Experience, Identity, Policy, Agency*, 121–39, New York: Columbia University Press.

Bruni, L. and P. L. Porta (2005), 'Introduction', in L. Bruni and P. L. Porta (eds), *Economics and Happiness*, 1–28, Oxford: Oxford University Press.

Bunzli, J. (2000), 'Autobiography in the House of Mirrors: The Paradox of Identity Reflected in the Solo Shows of Robert Lepage', in J. Donohoe Jr and J. Koustas (eds), *Theater Sans Frontières: Essays on the Dramatic Universe of Robert Lepage*, 21–41, East Lansing: Michigan State University Press.

Burelle, J. (2014), 'Staging Empathy's Limit Point: First Nations Theatre and the Challenges of Self Representation on a Settler-Stage Stage', in E. Hurley (ed.), *Theatres of Affect*, 246–62, Toronto: Playwrights Canada Press.

Butler, J. (2004a), *Undoing Gender*, New York: Routledge.

Butler, J. (2004b), *Precarious Life*, London: Verso.

Cahill, P. (2010), 'Falling into Extremity', in L. Gallagher and S. Raman (eds), *Knowing Shakespeare*, 82–101, Basingstoke: Palgrave Shakespeare Studies.

Carnicke, S. (2009), *Stanislavsky in Focus*, London: Routledge.

Carroll, N. (2011), 'On Some Affective Relations between Audiences and the Characters in Popular Fictions', in A. Coplan and P. Goldie (eds), *Empathy: Philosophical and Psychological Perspectives*, 162–84, Oxford: Oxford University Press.

Carter, J. (2015), 'Discarding Sympathy, Disrupting Catharsis: The Mortification of Indigenous Flesh as Survivance–Intervention', *Theatre Journal* 67 (3): 413–32.

Casey, M. (2004), *Creating Frames: Contemporary Indigenous Theatre 1967–1990*, St Lucia: University of Queensland Press.

Celant, G. (2001), *Marina Abramovic: Public Body Installations and Objects 1965–2001*, Milan: Edizioni Charta.

Chaturvedi, R. (2001), 'Interdisciplinarity: A Traditional Aspect of Indian Theatre', *Theatre Research International* 26 (2): 164–71.

Chatzichristodoulou, M. and R. Zerihan (2012), 'Introduction', in M. Chatzichristodoulou and R. Zerihan (eds), *Intimacy Across Visceral and Digital Performance*, 1–11, Basingstoke: Palgrave Macmillan.

Chaudhuri, U. (2014), 'Theorizing Ecocide: The "Theatre of Eco-Cruelty"', in U. Chaudhuri and S. Enelow (eds), *Research Theatre, Climate Change and the Ecocide Project: A Casebook*, 22–40, New York: Palgrave Macmillan.

Chekhov, A. (1991), *The Seagull*, in *Five Plays*, trans. R. Hingley, 65–115, Oxford: Oxford University Press.

Churchill, C. (1994), *The Skriker*, London: Nick Hern Books.

Churchill, C. (2012), *Love and Information*, London: Nick Hern Books.

Cless, D. (2012), 'Ecodirecting Canonical Plays', in W. Arons and T. May (eds), *Readings in Performance and Ecology*, 159–68, New York: Palgrave.

Clore, G. L. and K. Gasper (2000), 'Feeling Is Believing: Some Affective Influences on Belief', in N. Frijda, A. S. R. Manstead and S. Bem (eds), *Emotions and Beliefs*, 10–44, Cambridge: Cambridge University Press.

Clough, P. with J. Halley, eds (2007a), *The Affective Turn*, Durham: Duke University Press.

Clough, P. (2007b), 'Introduction', in P. Clough with J. Halley (eds), *The Affective Turn*, 1–33, Durham: Duke University Press.

Cody, G. (2003), 'Review of *To You, The Birdie! (Phèdre)*', *Theatre Journal* 55 (1): 173–5.

Cody, G. and E. Sprinchorn, eds (2007), *The Columbia Encyclopedia of Modern Drama*, Vols 1 and 2, New York: Columbia University Press.

Coplan, A. (2011), 'Understanding Empathy', in A. Coplan and P. Goldie (eds), *Empathy: Philosophical and Psychological Perspectives*, 3–18, Oxford: Oxford University Press.

Coplan, A. and P. Goldie, eds (2011a), *Empathy: Philosophical and Psychological Perspectives*, Oxford: Oxford University Press.

Coplan, A. and P. Goldie (2011b), 'Introduction', in A. Coplan and P. Goldie (eds), *Empathy: Philosophical and Psychological Perspectives*, ix–xlvii, Oxford: Oxford University Press.

Crew, R. (2013), '[...] *Needles and Opium*', *Toronto Star*, 24 November, E.2.

Cummings, L. (2016), *Empathy as Dialogue in Theatre and Performance*, London: Palgrave Macmillan for Springer.

Damasio, A. (2003), *Looking for Spinoza: Joy, Sorrow, and the Feeling Brain*, Orlando, FL: Harcourt.

Damasio, A. (2004), 'Emotions and Feelings: A Neurobiological Perspective', in A. Manstead, N. Frijda and A. Fischer (eds), *Feelings and Emotions*, 49–57, Cambridge: Cambridge University Press.

Defraeye, P. (2000), 'The Stage Body in Lepage's Musical Productions', in J. Donohoe Jr and J. Koustas (eds), *Theater sans Frontières: Essays on the Dramatic Universe of Robert Lepage*, 79–93, East Lansing: Michigan State University Press.

de Waal, F. (2009), *The Age of Empathy*, New York: Harmony Books.

Diamond, E. (2017), 'Feminism, Assemblage, and Performance: Kara Walker in Neoliberal Times', in E. Diamond, D. Varney and C. Amich (eds), *Performance, Feminism and Affect in Neoliberal Times*, 255–68, London: Springer Palgrave Macmillan.

Diamond, E., D. Varney and C. Amich (2017), 'Introduction', in E. Diamond, D. Varney and C. Amich (eds), *Performance, Feminism and Affect in Neoliberal Times*, ix–xiii, London: Springer Palgrave Macmillan.

Di Benedetto, S. (2010), *The Provocation of the Senses in Contemporary Theatre*, New York: Routledge.

Diderot, D. (1957), *The Paradox of Acting*, trans. W. H. Pollock, 11–71, New York: Hill and Wang.

Dixon, S. (2007), *Digital Performance*, Cambridge, MA: MIT Press.

Dolan, J. (2008), *Utopia in Performance*, Ann Arbor: The University of Michigan Press.

Doyle, J. (2013), *Hold It Against Me: Difficulty and Emotion in Contemporary Art*, Durham, NC: Duke University Press.

Dreysse, M. and F. Malzacher, eds (2008), *Experts of the Everyday: The Theatre of Rimini Protokoll*, Berlin: Alexander Verlag.

Duggan, P. (2012), *Trauma-Tragedy: Symptoms of Contemporary Performance*, Manchester: Manchester University Press.

Dumitriu, A. (2012), '*The Normal Flora Project*: Intimate Revelations in Art and Science', in M. Chatzichristodoulou and R. Zerihan (eds), *Intimacy across Visceral and Digital Performance*, 74–85, Basingstoke: Palgrave Macmillan.

Dundjerovic, A. (2009), *Robert Lepage*, London: Routledge.

Eckersall, P., H. Grehan and E. Scheer (2017), *New Media Dramaturgy*, London: Palgrave Macmillan.

Ekman, P. and R. Davidson, eds (1994a), *The Nature of Emotion*, New York: Oxford University Press.

Ekman, P. and R. Davidson (1994b), 'Afterword: Are There Basic Emotions?', in P. Ekman and R. Davidson (eds), *The Nature of Emotion*, 45–7, New York: Oxford University Press.

Empathy Museum (n.d.), http://www.empathymuseum.com, last accessed 8 May 2020.

Enelow, S. (2014), *Carla and Lewis*, in U. Chaudhuri and S. Enelow (eds), *Research Theatre, Climate Change and the Ecocide Project: A Casebook*, 87–116, New York: Palgrave Macmillan.

Escolme, B. (2014), *Emotional Excess on the Shakespearean Stage*, London: Bloomsbury.

Euripides (1967), *The Medea*, trans. R. Warner, in D. Grene and R. Lattimore, *Euripides 1*, 55–108, Chicago: The University of Chicago Press.

Euripides (1978), *Medea and Other Plays*, trans. P. Vellacott, 17–61, Harmondsworth: Penguin Books.

Euripides (1994), *Medea*, trans. K. McLeish and F. Raphael, London: Nick Hern.

Euripides (1997a), *Hippolytus*, trans. J. Morwood, 39–80, Oxford: Clarendon Press.

Euripides (1997b), *Hippolytos*, trans. F. Raphael and K. McLeish, in *Plays: Six*, 28–56, London: Bloomsbury Methuen Drama.

Evans, M. (2003), *Love: An Unromantic Discussion*, Cambridge: Polity.

Fahy, T. (2012), 'Peering behind the Curtain: An Introduction', in T. Fahy and K. King (eds), *Peering behind the Curtain: Disability, Illness and the Extraordinary Body in Contemporary Theater*, i–ix, New York: Routledge.

Feagin, S. (2012), 'Affects in Appreciation', in P. Goldie (ed.), *The Oxford Handbook of Philosophy of Emotion*, 635–50, Oxford: Oxford University Press.

Felski, R. and S. Fraiman (2012), 'Introduction', *New Literary History* 43 (3): v–xii.

Féral, J. (2009), 'The Dramatic Art of Robert Lepage: Fragments of Identity', *Contemporary Theatre Review* 19 (2): 143–54, trans. L. Wickes and R. Perron, http://dx.doi.org/10.1080/10486800902770804, accessed 20 July 2017.

Fisher, M. (2007), 'We've Really Upset Some Men', *The Guardian*, 7 August, https://www.theguardian.com/culture/2007/aug/07/edinburghfestival2007.edinburghfestival1

Fisher, P. (2002), *The Vehement Passions*, Princeton: Princeton University Press.

Flatley, J. (2008), *Affective Mapping*, Cambridge, MA: Harvard University Press.

Fortier, M. (1997), *Theory/Theatre*, London: Routledge.

Foster, S. (2010), *Choreographing Empathy*, London: Routledge.

Foucault, M. (1990), *The Use of Pleasure: The History of Sexuality*, Vol. 2, trans. R. Hurley, New York: Vintage Books.

Freshwater, H. (2009), *Theatre and Audience*, Basingstoke: Palgrave Macmillan.

Freud, S. (1914–16), 'Mourning and Melancholia', in S. Freud (ed.), *The Complete Psychological Works of Sigmund Freud*, Vol. xiv, ed. and trans. James Strachey, 243–58, London: The Hogarth Press.

Frijda, N. (1994), 'Emotions Require Cognitions: Even if Simple Ones', in P. Ekman and R. Davidson (eds), *The Nature of Emotion*, 197–202, New York: Oxford University Press.

Garde-Hansen, J. and K. Gorton (2013), *Emotion Online: Theorizing Affect on the Internet*, Basingstoke: Palgrave Macmillan.

Garey, A. I. and K. Hansen (2011), 'Introduction', in A. Garey and K. Hansen (eds), *At the Heart of Work and Family: Engaging the Ideas of Arlie Hochschild*, 1–14, New Brunswick: Rutgers University Press.

Ghosh, A. (2016), *The Great Derangement*, Chicago: The University of Chicago Press.

Goldie, P. (2000), *The Emotions: A Philosophical Exploration*, Oxford: Oxford University Press.

Goldie, P. (2011), 'Anti-Empathy', in A. Coplan and P. Goldie (eds), *Empathy: Philosophical and Psychological Perspectives*, 302–17, Oxford: Oxford University Press.

Goldie, P., ed. (2012a), *The Oxford Handbook of Philosophy of Emotion*, Oxford: Oxford University Press.

Goldie, P. (2012b), 'Introduction', in P. Goldie (ed.), *The Oxford Handbook of Philosophy of Emotion*, 1–13, Oxford: Oxford University Press.

Goldman, A. (2011), 'Two Routes to Empathy: Insights from Cognitive Neuroscience', in A. Coplan and P. Goldie (eds), *Empathy: Philosophical and Psychological Perspectives*, 31–44, Oxford: Oxford University Press.

Goldman, M. (1999), *Ibsen: The Dramaturgy of Fear*, New York: Columbia.

Goodall, J. (2008), *Stage Presence*, London: Routledge.

Gordon, M. (2000), 'Salvaging Strasberg at the Fin de Siècle', in D. Krasner (ed.), *Method Acting Reconsidered*, 43–60, New York: St Martin's Press.

Green, J. R. (1994), *Theatre in Ancient Greek Society*, London: Routledge.

Gregg, M. and G. Seigworth, eds (2010), *The Affect Theory Reader*, Durham: Duke University Press.

Grehan, H. (2009), *Performance, Ethics and Spectatorship in a Global Age*, Basingstoke: Palgrave Macmillan.

Grehan, H. and P. Eckersall, eds (2013), '*We're People Who Do Shows': Back to Back Theatre, Performance, Politics, Visibility*, Aberystwyth: Performance Research Books.

Hadley, B. (2014), *Disability, Public Space Performance and Spectatorship: Unconscious Performers*, Basingstoke: Palgrave Macmillan.

Hall, E. (2010), *Greek Tragedy: Suffering under the Sun*, Oxford: Oxford University Press.

Hardt, M. (2007), 'Foreword: What Affects Are Good For', in P. Clough (ed.) with J. Halley, *The Affective Turn*, ix–xiii, Durham: Duke University Press.

Harpin, A. and J. Foster (2014), 'Introduction: Locating Madness and Performance', in A. Harpin and J. Foster (eds), *Performance, Madness and Psychiatry: Isolated Acts*, 1–16, Basingstoke: Palgrave Macmillan.

Harré, R. and W. G. Parrott, eds (1996), *The Emotions: Social, Cultural and Biological Dimensions*, London: Sage.

Harrison, J. (1998), *Stolen*, Sydney: Currency Press.

Harvie, J. (2000), 'Transnationalism, Orientalism, and Cultural Tourism: *La Trilogie des Dragons* and *The Seven Streams of the River Ota*', in J. Donohoe Jr and J. Koustas (eds), *Theater sans Frontières: Essays on the Dramatic Universe of Robert Lepage*, 109–25, East Lansing: Michigan State University Press.

Hatfield, E., J. T. Cacioppo and Rapson, R. (1994), *Emotional Contagion*, Cambridge: Cambridge University Press.

Heathfield, A., ed. (2004), *Live: Art and Performance*, New York: Routledge.

Hetzler, E. (2007), 'Actors and Emotion in Performance', *Studies in Theatre and Performance* 28 (1): 59–78.

Highmore, B. (2017), *Cultural Feelings: Mood, Mediation and Cultural Politics*, London: Routledge.

Hochschild, A. R. (1983), *The Managed Heart*, Berkeley: University of California Press.

Holledge, J., J. Bollen, F. Helland and J. Tompkins (2016), *A Global Doll's House: Ibsen and Distant Visions*, London: Palgrave Macmillan.

Howard, J. (1994), *The Stage and Social Struggle in Early Modern England*, London: Routledge.

Hughes, E. (2015), 'Maternal Practice and Maternal Presence in Jane Harrison's *Stolen*', *Outskirts: Feminisms along the Edge*, 33: 1–17, http://www.outskirts.arts.uwa.edu.au/volumes/volume-33/hughes, accessed 10 November 2015.

Hurley, E. (2010), *Theatre and Feeling*, Basingstoke: Palgrave Macmillan.

Hurley, E. (2014), 'Introduction: Theatre Matters', in E. Hurley (ed.), *Theatres of Affect*, 1–12, Toronto: Playwrights Canada Press.

Ibsen, H. (1982), *A Doll's House*, in *Plays: Two*, trans. M. Meyer, 23–104, London: Eyre Methuen.

James, W. (1984), '*From* What Is an Emotion?', in C. Calhoun and R. C. Solomon (eds), *What Is an Emotion?*, 127–41, New York: Oxford University Press.

James, W. with C. Lange (1967), *The Emotions*, New York: Hafner Publishing.

Jensen, K. A. and M. L. Wallace (2015), 'Introduction – Facing Emotions', *PMLA* 130 (5) October: 1249–68.

Johnston, K. (2016), *Disability Theatre and Modern Drama*, London: Bloomsbury.

Kane, S. (2002), *Phaedra's Love*, London: Bloomsbury Methuen Drama.

Kaplan, E. A. (2011), 'Empathy and Trauma Culture', in A. Coplan and P. Goldie (eds), *Empathy: Philosophical and Psychological Perspectives*, 255–76, Oxford: Oxford University Press.

Kastan, D. S., ed. (2006), *The Oxford Encyclopedia of British Literature*, Oxford: Oxford University Press.

Kear, A. (2013), *Theatre and Event: Staging the European Century*, Basingstoke: Palgrave Macmillan.

Kelleher, J. (2004), 'The Suffering of Images', in A. Heathfield (ed.), *Live: Art and Performance*, 190–5, New York: Routledge.

Kemp, R. (2012), *Embodied Acting: What Neuroscience Tells Us about Acting*, London: Routledge.

Kieran, M. (2012), 'Emotions, Art, and Immorality', in P. Goldie (ed.), *The Oxford Handbook of Philosophy of Emotions*, 681–703, Oxford: Oxford University Press.

Knowles, R. (2004), *Reading the Material Theatre*, Cambridge: Cambridge University Press.

Komporaly, J. (2006), *Staging Motherhood*, Basingstoke: Palgrave Macmillan.

Kondo, D. (2000), '(Re) Visions of Race: Contemporary Race Theory and the Cultural Politics of Racial Crossover in Documentary Theatre', *Theatre Journal* 52 (1): 81–107.

Konijn, E. (2000), *Acting Emotions: Shaping Emotions on Stage*, trans. B. Leach with D. Chambers, Amsterdam: Amsterdam University Press.

Krasner, D. (2000), 'I Hate Strasberg: Method Bashing in the Academy', in D. Krasner (ed.), *Method Acting Reconsidered*, 3–39, New York: St Martin's Press.

Kritzer, A. (1991), *The Plays of Caryl Churchill*, Basingstoke: Palgrave Macmillan.

Kuntsman, A. (2012), 'Introduction', in A. Karatzogianni and A. Kuntsman (eds), *Digital Cultures and the Politics of Emotion: Feelings, Affect and Technological Change*, 1–17, Basingstoke: Palgrave Macmillan.

Lalonde, M. (n.d.), *Speak White*, trans. A. Herring, https://www.everything2.com/index.pl?node_id=738881, accessed 30 December 2019.

Lan, Y. L. (2013), 'Intercultural Rhythm in Yohangza's Dream', in S. Bennett and C. Carson (eds), *Shakespeare beyond English*, 87–91, Cambridge: Cambridge University Press.

Lange, C. and W. James (1967), *The Emotions*, New York: Hafner Publishing.

Lazarus, R. (1994), 'Appraisal: The Long and the Short of It', in P. Ekman and R. Davidson (eds), *The Nature of Emotion*, 208–15, New York: Oxford University Press.

Lehmann, H.-T. (2007), *Postdramatic Theatre*, trans. K. Jürs-Munby, London: Routledge.

Lehmann, H.-T. (2016), *Tragedy and Dramatic Theatre*, trans. E. Butler, London: Routledge.

Lepecki, A. and S. Banes (2007), 'Introduction: The Performance of the Senses', in S. Banes and A. Lepecki (eds), *The Senses in Performance*, 1–7, New York: Routledge.

Leroux, P. and C. Batson, eds (2016), *Cirque Global*, Montreal & Kingston: McGill-Queen's University Press.

Li, Q. (1960), *The Chalk Circle*, in B. H. Clark (ed.), *World Drama*, 227–58, New York: Dover Publications, author not attributed in this version.

Liu, S. (2017), 'Towards a Chinese School of Performance and Directing: Jiao Juyin', in J. Pitches and S. Aquilina (eds), *Stanislavsky in the World*, 149–65, London: Bloomsbury Methuen Drama.

Lomas, T. (2019), *Happiness – Found in Translation: A Glossary of Joy from around the World*, New York: TarcherPerigee.

Looking for a Miracle (2008), [Film] Dir. Reiner Moritz, New York: Lorber HT Digital.

Luckhurst, M. (2015), *Caryl Churchill*, London: Routledge.

Luckhurst, M. and P. Tait (2019), 'Drama', in J. Davidson and J. Damousi (eds), *A Cultural History of the Emotions in the Modern and Postmodern Age*, Vol. 6, 73–90, London: Bloomsbury.

Lupton, D. (1998), *The Emotional Self*, London: Sage.

Lutz, C. and L. Abu-Lughod, eds (1990), *Language and the Politics of Emotions*, Cambridge: Cambridge University Press.

Lydon, J. (2016), *Photography, Humanitarianism, Empire*, London: Bloomsbury.

Mabou Mines' Dollhouse (2008), Dir. Lee Breuer, New York: Lorber HT Digital.

Mabou Mines (n.d.), https://www.maboumines.org/production/mabou-mines-dollhouse/, last accessed 10 May 2020.

Machon, J. (2013), *Immersive Theatres: Intimacy and Immediacy in Contemporary Performance*, Basingstoke: Palgrave Macmillan.

Malague, R. (2012), *An Actress Prepares: Women and 'the Method'*, London: Routledge.

Marina Abramovic: The Artist Is Present (2012), [Film] Dir. M. Akers, HBO Documentary Films, Submarine Deluxe, accessed through Kanopy Film.

Marshall, H. R. (2011), 'Saxon Violence and Social Decay in Sarah Kane's *Phaedra's Love* and Tony Harrison's *Prometheus*', *Helios* 38 (2): 165–79.

Marx, K. (1975), *Early Writings*, trans. R. Livingstone and G. Benton, Harmondsworth: Penguin Books.

Massumi, B. (2002), *Parables for the Virtual: Movement, Affect, Sensation*, Durham: Duke University Press.

Matravers, D. (2012), 'Expression in the Arts', in P. Goldie (ed.), *The Oxford Handbook of Philosophy of Emotion*, 617–34, Oxford: Oxford University Press.

McConachie, B. and F. E. Hart, eds (2006), *Performance and Cognition*, London: Routledge.

McFee, G. (2011), 'Empathy: Interpersonal vs Artistic?', in A. Coplan and P. Goldies (eds), *Empathy: Philosophical and Psychological Perspectives*, 185–208, Oxford: Oxford University Press.

Meek, R. (2012), 'Introduction: Shakespeare and the Culture of Emotion', *Shakespeare* 8 (3): 279–85.

Meineck, P. (2017), *Theatrocracy: Greek Drama, Cognition, and the Imperative for Theatre*, London: Routledge.

Meisner, S. and D. Longwell (1987), *Sanford Meisner on Acting*, New York: Vintage Books.

Merlin, B. (2003), *Konstantin Stanislavsky*, London: Routledge.

Meyerhold, V. (1969), 'The Naturalistic Theatre and the Theatre of Mood', in E. Brun (trans. and ed.), *Meyerhold on Theatre*, trans. E. Braun, 23–34, New York: Hill and Wang.

Mishra, P. (2017), *Age of Anger: A History of the Present*, New York: Farrar, Straus and Giroux.

Morris, L. F. (2012), 'Acting without Limits: Profiles of Three Physically Disabled Performers', in T. Fahy and K. King (eds), *Peering behind the Curtain: Disability, Illness and the Extraordinary Body in Contemporary Theater*, 95–106, New York: Routledge.

Morton, A. (2013), *Emotion and Imagination*, Cambridge: Polity.

Mumford, M. (2009), *Bertolt Brecht*, London: Routledge.

Mumford, M. (2013), 'Rimini Protokoll's Reality Theatre and Intercultural Encounter: Towards an Ethical Art of Partial Proximity', *Contemporary Theatre Review* 23 (2): 153–65.

Neuerburg-Denzer, U. (2014), 'High Emotion – Rasaboxes in the Emo Lab: Emotion Training for Actors in the Twenty-first Century', in E. Hurley (ed.), *Theatres of Affect*, 76–95, Toronto: Playwrights Canada Press.

Nielsen, L. (2012), 'Introduction: Heterotopic Transformations, The (Il) Liberal Neoliberal', in L. Nielsen and P. Ybarra (eds),

Neoliberalism and Global Theatres: Performance Permutations, 1–21, Basingstoke: Palgrave Macmillan.

Nussbaum, M. (2005), 'Mill between Aristotle and Bentham', in L. Bruni and P. L. Porta (eds), *Economics and Happiness*, 170–83, Oxford: Oxford University Press.

O'Reilly, A. (2010), 'Introduction', in A. O'Reilly (ed.), *Twenty-First Century Motherhood: Experience, Identity, Policy, Agency*, 1–20, New York: Columbia University Press.

Parker-Starbuck, J. (2011), *Cyborg Theatre: Corporeal/Technological Intersections in Multimedia Performance*, Basingstoke: Palgrave Macmillan.

Parkinson, B., A. H. Fischer and A. S. R. Manstead (2005), *Emotion in Social Relations*, New York: Psychology Press.

Paster, G. (2004), *Humoring the Body: Emotions and the Shakespearean Stage*, Chicago: The University of Chicago Press.

Paterson, E. (2015), *The Contemporary American Monologue*, London: Bloomsbury.

Payne, N. (2014), *Incognito*, London: Nick Hern Books.

Phelan, P. (1993), *Unmarked*, London: Routledge.

Phelan, P. (2001), 'Survey', in H. Reckitt (ed.), *Art and Feminism*, 14–49, London: Phaidon Press.

Pitches, J. and S. Aquilina, eds (2017), *Stanislavsky in the World*, London: Bloomsbury Methuen Drama.

Plato (1972), *The Republic of Plato*, trans. F. M. Cornford, Oxford: Oxford University Press.

Price, C. (2015), *Emotion*, Cambridge: Polity Press.

Prynne, W. (1633), *Histrio-Mastix: The Players Scourge*, London: Michael Sparke.

Racine, J. (1993), *Phaedra*, in B. Worthen (ed.), *The HBJ Anthology of Drama*, trans. R. C. Knight, 305–20, Fort Worth, Texas: Harcourt Brace.

Rancière, J. (2014), *The Politics of Aesthetics: The Distribution of the Sensible*, trans. G. Rockhill, London: Bloomsbury.

Ratcliffe, M. (2012), 'The Phenomenology of Mood and the Meaning of Life', in P. Goldie (ed.), *The Oxford Handbook of Philosophy of Emotion*, 349–71, Oxford: Oxford University Press.

Ridout, N. (2006), *State Fright, Animals and Other Theatrical Problems*, Cambridge: Cambridge University Press.

Rimini Protokoll (2016), http://rimini-protokoll.de, last accessed 9 January 2019.

Rix, R. (1998), 'Learning Alba Emoting', *Theatre Topics* 8 (1): 55–71.

Roach, J. (1985), *The Player's Passion*, Newark: The University of Delaware Press.

Roberts, R. (2003), *Emotions: An Essay in Aid of Moral Psychology*, Cambridge: Cambridge University Press.

Robinson, J. (2012), 'Emotional Responses to Music: What Are They? How Do They Work? and Are They Relevant to Aesthetic Appreciation?', in P. Goldie (ed.), *The Oxford Handbook of Philosophy of Emotion*, 651–80, Oxford: Oxford University Press.

Ruddick, S. (2009), 'On Maternal Thinking', *Women's Studies Quarterly* 37 (3 and 4): 305–8.

Savran, D. (1986), *The Wooster Group, 1975–1985: Breaking the Rules*, Ann Arbor: UMI Research.

Schafer, E. (2009), 'Introduction', in E. Schafer (ed.), *Twelfth Night*, 1–78, Cambridge: Cambridge University Press.

Schafer, E. (2013), 'Technicolour *Twelfth Night*', in S. Bennett and C. Carson (eds), *Shakespeare beyond English*, 68–71, Cambridge: Cambridge University Press.

Schechner, R. (2001), 'Rasaesthetics', *TDR: The Drama Review* 45 (3): 27–50.

Schramm, H. and B. S. Michieli (2009), 'Pathos and Melancholy: Rethinking "Theatre" in Times of Doubt', *Theatre Research International* 34 (3): 278–93.

Senior, A. (2014), 'Relics of Bioart: Ethics and Messianic Aesthetics in Performance Documentation', *Theatre Journal* 66 (2): 183–205.

Shakespeare, W. (2009a), *Twelfth Night*, ed. E. Schafer, Cambridge: Cambridge University Press.

Shakespeare, W. (2009b), *King Lear*, Basingstoke: Macmillan.

Shakespeare, W. (2019), *Hamlet*, ed. Philip Edwards, Cambridge: Cambridge University Press.

Shaughnessy, N., ed. (2013), *Affective Performance and Cognitive Science*, London: Bloomsbury.

Shirley, D. (2018), 'Stanislavski and Contemporary Directing Practice', in P. Tait (ed.), *The Great European Theatre Directors: Antoine, Stanislavski, St Denis*, Vol. 1, 113–33, London: Bloomsbury.

Shusterman, R. (2012), 'Thought in the Strenuous Mood', *New Literary History* 43 (3): 433–54.

Shweder, R. (2004), 'Deconstructing the Emotions for the Sake of Comparative Research', in A. Manstead, N. Frijda and A. Fischer (eds), *Feelings and Emotions*, 81–97, Cambridge: Cambridge University Press.

Smith. A. D. (1999), *Fires in the Mirror*, New York: Random House.

Solga, K. (2019), *Theory for Theatre Studies: Space*, London: Bloomsbury.

Sommer, E. (2002), '*To You, the Birdie!*: A CurtainUp Review', http://www.curtainup.com/toyouthebirdie.html, last accessed 19 April 2017.

Sprinchorn, E. (2007), 'Realism', in G. Cody and E. Sprinchorn (eds), *The Columbia Encyclopedia of Modern Drama*, 1124, New York: Colombia University Press.

Stanislavski, K. (2010), *An Actor's Work*, trans. and ed. J. Benedetti, London: Routledge.

Stanislavsky, K. (1952), *The Seagull Produced by Stanislavsky/The Seagull by Anton Chekhov: Production Score for the Moscow Art Theatre*, ed. S. D. Balukhaty, trans. D. Magarshack, London: Dennis Dobson.

Steiner, G. (1984), *Antigones*, Oxford: Clarendon Press.

Stendhal's Vertigo (2015), [Film] Dir. A. Taillant, France: Wendigo Films, distributed by Andana Films.

Sternfeld, J. (2006), *The Megamusical*, Bloomington: Indiana University Press.

Stevens, L. (2016), *Anti-War Theatre after Brecht*, London: Palgrave Macmillan.

Stevens, L. (2018), 'Live after Extinction', *Performance Research* 23 (3): 27–36.

Stevens, L., P. Tait and D. Varney (2018), 'Introduction: "Street Fighters and Philosophers" Traversing Ecofeminisms', in L. Stevens, P. Tait and D. Varney (eds), *Feminist Ecologies: Changing Environments in the Anthropocene*, 1–22, London: Palgrave Macmillan.

Stinespring, L. M. (2000), 'Just Be Yourself: Derrida, Difference, and the Meisner Technique', in D. Krasner (ed.), *Method Acting Reconsidered*, 97–109, New York: St Martin's Press.

Tait, P. (2002), *Performing Emotions*, Aldershot: Ashgate/Routledge.

Tait, P. (2012), *Wild and Dangerous Performances*, Basingstoke: Palgrave Macmillan.

Tait, P. (2015), 'Love, Fear and Climate Change: Emotions in Drama and Performance', *Publication of the Modern Languages Association of America (PMLA)* 130 (5): 1501–5.

Tait, P. (2018), 'Introduction to Volume 1: Directors Transforming Realism', in P. Tait (ed.), *The Great European Theatre Directors: Antoine, Stanislavski, St Denis*, Vol. 1, 7–16, London: Bloomsbury.

Tait, P. (forthcoming), *Forms of Emotion*, London: Routledge.

Tait, P. and J.-S. Shim, eds (2006), 'Theatre, Emotions and Interculturalism', *Australasian Drama Studies* 49.

Taylor, M. (2012), *Music Theatre, Realism and Entertainment*, Farnham: Ashgate/Routledge.

Taylor, P. (1997), 'Caucasian Chalk Circle RNT, London Review', *The Independent*, 23 April, https://www.independent.co.uk/arts-entertainment/caucasian-chalk-circle-rnt-london-review-1268727.html, accessed 8 January 2018.

The 7 Faces of Robert Lepage (1997), [Film] Dir. Michel Duchesne, Montreal: Cinema 3180 BE.

Thompson, J. (2011), *Performance Affects*, Basingstoke: Palgrave Macmillan.

Tomkins, S. (1995), *Shame and Its Sisters*, ed. E. K. Sedgwick and A. Frank, Durham: Duke University Press.

Toporkov, V. O. (1998), *Stanislavski in Rehearsal*, trans. C. Edwards, New York: Routledge.

Trezise, B. (2014), *Performing Feeling in Cultures of Memory*, Basingstoke: Palgrave Macmillan.

Umiltà, M. A. (2017), 'The "Mirror Mechanism" and Motor Behaviour', in C. Falletti, G. Sofia and V. Jacono (eds), *Theatre and Cognitive Neuroscience*, 15–22, London: Bloomsbury Methuen Drama.

van der Tuin, I. and R. Dolphijn (2010), 'The Transversality of New Materialism', *Women: A Cultural Review* 21 (2): 153–71.

Varney, D. (2017), 'Minor Characters in the NT Medea', *Skene* 3(1): 165–79.

Villalobos, A. (2010), 'Mothering in Fear: How Living in an Insecure-Feeling World Affects Parenting', in A. O'Reilly (ed.), *Twenty-First-Century Motherhood: Experience, Identity, Policy, Agency*, 57–71, New York: Columbia University Press.

Vineberg, S. (1991), *Method Actors*, New York: Schirmer Macmillan Books.

Wald, C. (2007), *Hysteria, Trauma and Melancholia: Performative Maladies in Contemporary Anglophone Drama*, Basingstoke: Palgrave Macmillan.

Washburn, A. (2015), *Mr. Burns and Other Plays*, New York: Theatre Communications Group.

Waters, S. (2006), 'Sarah Kane: From Terror to Trauma', in M. Luckhurst (ed.), *A Companion to Modern British and Irish Drama 1800–2005*, 371–82, Malden, MA: Blackwell Publishing.

Welton, M. (2012), *Feeling Theatre*, Basingstoke: Palgrave Macmillan.

Whyman, R. (2008), *The Stanislavsky System of Acting*, Cambridge: Cambridge University Press.

Wiles, D. (1997), *Tragedy in Athens*, Cambridge: Cambridge University Press.

Williams, R. (1977), *Marxism and Literature*, Oxford: Oxford University Press.

Wolf, S. E. (2011), *Changed for Good: A Feminist History of the Broadway Musical*, New York: Oxford University Press.

Woodworth, C. (2010), 'The Abject of My Affection: The Erotics of Stepmotherhood in Sarah Kane's *Phaedre's Love* and the Wooster Group's *To You, The Birdie! (Phèdre)*', in B. Osnes and A. Andes (eds), *Essays and Scripts on How Mothers Are Portrayed in the Theater*, 133–55, Lewiston, New York: Edwin Mellen Press.

Wright, T. (1620), *The Passions of the Minde in Generall*, London: Anne Helme.

Zarrilli, P. (2009), *Psychophysical Acting: An Intercultural Approach after Stanislavski*, London: Routledge.

Zerihan, R. (2010), 'Revisiting Catharsis in Contemporary Live Art Practice: Kira O'Reilly's Evocative Skin Works', *Theatre Research International* 35 (1): 32–42.

INDEX